Recipes *from my* Mother
for my Daughter

LISA FAULKNER

Recipes from my Mother for my Daughter

First published in Great Britain in 2012
by Simon & Schuster UK Ltd
A CBS Company

Text Copyright © Lisa Faulkner 2012
Design Copyright © Simon & Schuster 2012

1 3 5 7 9 10 8 6 4 2

Simon & Schuster Illustrated Books
Simon & Schuster UK Ltd
222 Gray's Inn Road
London
WC1X 8HB

www.simonandschuster.co.uk

Simon & Schuster Australia, Sydney

Simon & Schuster India, New Delhi

A CIP catalogue for this book is available
from the British Library

ISBN 978-0-85720-616-9

Editorial Director: Francine Lawrence
Senior Commissioning Editor: Nicky Hill
Project Editor: Abi Waters
Designer: Miranda Harvey
Photographer: Chris Terry
Home Economists: Richard Harris and Abi Fawcett
Stylist: Polly Webb-Wilson
Hair and Make-up: Justine Wade
Commercial Director: Ami Richards
Production Manager: Katherine Thornton

Colour reproduction by Dot Gradations Ltd, UK
Printed and bound in China

Notes on the recipes

Both metric and imperial measurements have been
given in all recipes. Use one set of measurements only
and not a mixture of both.

Spoon measures are level and 1 tablespoon = 15 ml,
1 teaspoon = 5 ml.

Preheat ovens before use and cook on the centre shelf
wherever possible. If using a fan oven, reduce the heat
by 10–20°C, but check with your handbook.

Medium free-range eggs have been used unless
otherwise stated.

I tend to use unsalted butter and light olive oil in my
cooking, but use whichever sort you normally use.

This book contains recipes made with nuts. Those
with known allergic reactions to nuts and nut
derivatives, pregnant and breast-feeding women and
very young children should avoid these dishes.

Contents

Introduction

My food journey

My earliest memories of my mum Julie, are of her cooking. I can close my eyes and swamp my senses. I can smell the wonderful aromas as if they were drifting up to my childhood bedroom. Clear as a bell, I can hear the knife on the chopping board and her wedding ring tinkling against her glass rolling pin as she shaped pastry... the glass rolling pin that is now in my possession, and my secret weapon in the art of pastry!

I was never allowed to call Mummy just 'Mum', she was always called Mummy. If I referred to her as Mum now she would be turning in her grave! Therefore, when I refer to her in this way in the book it's not pretentious or posh, it's just that's who she was to me.

Where it all began

I loved to sit at the kitchen table watching in awe as my mum made profiteroles, chicken tarragon, beef Wellington and the most beautiful birthday and Christmas cakes for family and friends and friends that were like family. What has stayed with me more than anything though, is the taste of her food. Whatever she made was delicious. She had a gift for making everything taste just right. To me, she was magic. It's no surprise really, she learnt from the best in my opinion.

Nanna, my mum's mum, spoilt us rotten. We cooked with her nearly every weekend. Drop scones, soda bread, rock cakes and cola floats. Every Sunday her house was filled with the smell of pastry and roast lamb. Nothing was ever wasted in her kitchen and leftovers all had their uses in recipes later on. What Nanna doesn't know about pastry and baking isn't worth knowing – she passed on her secrets to my mum and, I hope now, to my sister and I.

We were especially lucky as both of our grandmothers were excellent cooks. Nanna is still with us but my grandma Betty died years ago (we were never allowed to call her grandma because she thought she was too young to be one!). My memories of Betty are of idyllic weekends spent in West Wittering, a beautiful little village on the Sussex coast. We were either at the beach hut (in all weathers!) with a tin of homemade jam tarts and a corned beef sandwich, or running around her garden collecting 'windfalls' to be eaten later that day in a crumble. Her jams were memorable but she was most famous for her marmalade (see page 194), my dad's favourite.

I was 16 when my mum died, two years older than my sister. Words can't express just how horrendous that time was. It was devastating to our family, and our worlds and lives were changed forever. Our dad was truly amazing, becoming all things to both his daughters. Being the oldest, I took it upon myself to assume the role of the mummy. I'd iron my dad's shirts, get our school uniforms ready and, with the help of my sister, make the dinner. Our dad never asked or expected this from us, in fact he bought a book called *How to Boil an Egg* to help him learn the kitchen basics. I cooked the simple, everyday recipes I'd picked up along the way. Family meals like shepherd's pie, lasagne, roast chicken and toad in the hole, stuff that would now be labelled 'comfort food'. And I suppose, in a way, that makes sense. Thinking back, I realise the process of preparing and making food gave me a focus. Cooking made me feel like I had a purpose in a world that had just crumbled around me. It's funny to think that the first dish I served on *Celebrity MasterChef* ended up being chicken and mash... the food that makes me feel good.

My rock

Over the years my relationship with food has, like any strong marriage, had its fair share of ups and downs. As a model in my teens I lived on fresh air and green beans, and then as a young actress on vodka and soda. I spent a lot of time away from home, travelling the world and never knowing where my next job would take me. Wherever I was though, my heart was always firmly at home. My family became even more of a rock for me, and when my sister married and had children (while I was still running around partying and splitting up with boyfriends) my favourite thing was to invite everyone round for a Sunday roast. Over dinner, I'd listen to their stories, laughing, reminiscing, feeling safe and warm... and full! All of us together, the children playing, eating, love and food – a great combination. I believe it's true what they say, the family that eats together, stays together.

A family of my own

Later on when I had a husband of my own and we were trying to start a family, I fell in love with food all over again. We tried hard (believe me!) but eventually, and after many heartbreaks, we had to accept that we weren't going to be able to have children naturally. But we were both absolutely desperate for kids and weren't going to give up, so we set off on the long, hard journey of fertility treatment. Months of various pills, procedures and treatments lay ahead. We endured three shattering failed IVF attempts. It wasn't an easy time for us and I don't know if it was the drugs or the hormones or the fact that I was actively being encouraged to put on weight, but I found all I wanted to do was bake. And bake. It took my mind off things. Cakes, banana bread, chocolate brownies, apple pies, macaroons... food that made me feel better. I stood in the kitchen, rolling off endless batches and dispersed them to family and friends to enjoy.

They say every snowflake lands in the right place and when we met our daughter, we knew she had come home. She is beautiful in every way. After 11 nerve-shredding, but wonderful months of fostering, we finally adopted Billie and my dream of being a mum that I'd thought was never going to come true was finally granted.

Now we have a house filled with noise and toys and pink things and the kitchen is at its heart. Because now I have to cook for her! And cooking for kids isn't easy. Kids know what they like and they like what they know. They're fussy little things and trying to keep them happy at the dinner table can be a minefield.

I have two main things to share on the subject of cooking for kids that I've learnt by adapting my cooking so my little girl enjoys it, too. The first is flavour. If you can make a meal that's all about the taste, then you can save yourself from the mind-numbing cycle of cooking the same old thing with the same old ingredients, time and time again. 'Mum food' doesn't have to be boring. And it doesn't have to take forever to make.

The second is by far the most important as far as I'm concerned. Cook with your kids! Include them and involve them in what they're eating. Get them interested. Show them what goes in. Let them taste it. Let them stir it. Let them get dirty. Let them use the glass rolling pin! It's more than likely they'll love it. I loved it, and now so does my daughter. Just like me when I was a little girl, Billie's always at her mummy's elbow in the kitchen. Whenever she and I cook together, whatever it is we are making, she always makes sure that we 'sprinkle it with a bit of love' before it can go in the oven. I think everything tastes better when it's made with love.

My MasterChef experience

I never dreamt that I would become the winner of *Celebrity MasterChef*. I honestly thought I'd turn up, have a lovely day meeting John and Gregg and then be sent packing! I had to fight to believe in myself, so I gritted my teeth and worked as hard as I could to learn and improve. And I did, I learned so much. I learnt things and methods that I knew I'd never use at home, but I've taken elements from them to cook easy, everyday, interesting meals. Food that makes my family and I feel good.

On the evening of the final show, my godparents called me to tell me that I'd 'beaten Mummy'. They said that hers had been the best food they had ever tasted, but now surely mine must be. I thanked them very much for their lovely words, but I know they were just being kind. My mother is my MasterChef and always will be. This book is dedicated to her.

I have been told since winning *Celebrity MasterChef* that after seeing me on the show I sent people into their kitchens, and that I inspired them to cook. I love that! I hope my recipes will tell a story and inspire you to try something different. I want you to experiment with these recipes, try them, substitute ingredients, posh them up, dress them down.

Have fun, because most of all, I want you to enjoy them.

x

Spring

Goat's cheese quenelles
with pear & walnut salad

I first made Goat's cheese quenelles for Sebastian Coe on *Celebrity MasterChef* – I was terrified, but he loved them! I don't know if what scared me most was Seb Coe or the word 'quenelle'! It's basically just a word for an oval spoon shape. Don't worry if you can't do it, just shape them into balls instead. I think these quenelles are so light and the cheese really brings out the flavour of the pear. A winning combination all round.

Serves 4

For the quenelles

500 g (1 lb) goat's cheese

flour, for rolling

1 egg, beaten

100 g (3½ oz) dried breadcrumbs

vegetable or sunflower oil, for deep-frying

For the salad & dressing

1 tablespoon olive oil

1 heaped teaspoon honey

2 pears, quartered lengthways

1 tablespoon walnut oil

1 tablespoon white wine vinegar

50 g (2 oz) rocket

50 g (2 oz) watercress

50 g (2 oz) walnuts, lightly toasted, broken

salt and freshly ground black pepper

To make the quenelles, put the goat's cheese in a mixing bowl and use a wooden spoon to beat it gently and soften it until it is more pliable.

Put the flour, beaten egg and breadcrumbs in 3 separate shallow bowls ready to make the quenelles.

Use 2 spoons to shape the goat's cheese into quenelle shapes. Roll each one in the flour, then the beaten egg and then the breadcrumbs. Ensure they are fully coated and tap a little to shake off any excess.

Heat the oil to about 180°C (350°F). To test that the oil is ready, drop a cube of bread into the oil and if it turns golden after 20–30 seconds then the oil is ready. Deep-fry the quenelles for 3–4 minutes or until the breadcrumbs are golden.

Meanwhile, make the salad dressing. Mix the olive oil and honey in a small jar, close the lid and shake until fully mixed.

Heat a griddle pan and brush the pears with the oil and honey mixture and cook them on the griddle for 2–3 minutes on each side or until just slightly coloured.

Add the walnut oil, white wine vinegar and some salt and pepper to the jar of oil and honey and shake to mix.

Mix the salad leaves and walnuts together in a bowl and toss in the shaken dressing. Arrange the dressed salad on serving plates, topped with the griddled pear slices and the cheese quenelles and serve immediately.

Mummy's spinach & cream cheese quiche

I'm very affected by the weather – I wish I wasn't but I am, and I remember my mum being the same. As soon as the days started getting lighter all our moods lifted, windows would be opened, daffodils bought and the heart-warming food that kept us going through winter would be replaced with new potatoes, salads, fish and of course, quiche. I love that my mum made her own quiches, they were always so light and tasty. This one is my favourite and would always be taken on picnics as the spring days got warm enough to eat outside.

Serves 4

1 x 375 g (12 oz) pack of ready-made shortcrust pastry or make your own (see recipe, page 39)

25 g (1 oz) butter, plus extra for greasing

flour, for dusting

1 small onion, sliced

1 garlic clove, finely chopped

about 10 cherry tomatoes, halved

200 g (7 oz) spinach (I always use baby leaf)

a squeeze of lemon juice

300 g (10 oz) cream cheese

2 eggs

a pinch of nutmeg

salt and freshly ground black pepper

a bunch of watercress, to serve

Preheat the oven to 180°C (350°F), gas mark 4. Grease a 23 cm (9 inch) loose-bottomed tart tin or alternatively make individual tarts using four 12 cm (5 inch) tart tins.

Roll the pastry out on a lightly floured worksurface to about 5 mm (¼ inch) thick. Use it to line the flan tin(s). Line the pastry with baking paper and then top with baking beans or rice and bake blind in the preheated oven for 25 minutes. Remove the beans or rice and lining paper.

Meanwhile, heat a large frying pan and melt the butter. Add the sliced onion and cook for 3–4 minutes until softened. Add the garlic, tomatoes, spinach, lemon juice and season to taste. Continue to cook for 5 minutes, then take off the heat.

Mix the cream cheese, eggs and nutmeg together in a bowl. Pour this into the spinach mixture and stir to combine. Check the seasoning again and then pour the mixture into the baked flan case. Bake in the preheated oven for about 20 minutes for a large quiche, or 12–15 minutes for individual ones, until golden and firm on top. Serve warm or cold with a watercress salad.

Mushroom & asparagus risotto

Risotto is one of those things that if done right is delicious – however, I've had many a disappointing one in restaurants, so much so that I never wanted to attempt one myself! With my new-found confidence in cooking I decided to bite the bullet. I think the trick is when you first start making it you need to add stock a little at a time, keep stirring and keep watching it. This is a really creamy risotto despite not having any cream in it.

Serves 4

125 g (4 oz) unsalted butter

200 g (7 oz) mixed mushrooms, sliced

1 onion, chopped

1 garlic clove, chopped

200 g (7 oz) arborio rice

750 ml (1¼ pints) warm vegetable stock

200 g (7 oz) asparagus, sliced

100 g (3½ oz) baby leaf spinach

50 g (2 oz) Parmesan cheese, grated, plus extra shavings to finish

good-quality olive oil, for drizzling

salt and freshly ground black pepper

Heat 50 g (1 oz) of the butter in a large heavy-based frying pan and cook the mushrooms for about 3 minutes. Use a slotted spoon to transfer them to a plate and keep warm.

In the same pan, gently fry the onion and garlic in the rest of the butter for a further 5 minutes.

Add the rice and cook for 3–4 minutes over a low heat, making sure all of the grains are coated in butter.

Slowly add the warm stock, a ladleful at a time, stirring continuously. Wait until the liquid has been absorbed by the rice before adding another ladleful of stock. Increase the heat to high now and keep stirring and adding ladles of stock. After about 15 minutes the rice will be cooked and you will have a beautifully creamy risotto.

Add the asparagus, cook for a further 3 minutes, then add the cooked mushrooms, spinach and the Parmesan and mix through the risotto so that the spinach wilts. Season to taste.

Serve in bowls topped with some Parmesan shavings and a drizzle of olive oil.

Remember, lots of stirring, lots of heat!

Arancini

My favourite thing about making risotto is using the leftovers to make arancini. If I go to a restaurant and they are on the menu I have to have them. They are, in my mind, the best thing you can make using leftovers!

Makes about 8

500 g (1 lb) leftover risotto

75 g (3 oz) mozzarella, cubed

flour, for rolling

1 egg, beaten

100 g (3½ oz) dried breadcrumbs or polenta

vegetable or sunflower oil, for deep-frying

Take about 2 tablespoons of the risotto mixture in your hand to make a flat patty. Press a cube of mozzarella into the middle, then mould the risotto into a ball completely encompassing the mozzarella.

Put the flour, beaten egg and breadcrumbs or polenta in 3 separate shallow bowls. Roll each ball in the flour, then the beaten egg and then the breadcrumbs or polenta. Transfer to the fridge to chill and firm for about 20 minutes.

Heat the oil to 180°C (350°F). To test that the oil is ready, drop a cube of bread into the oil, if it turns golden after 20–30 seconds then the oil is ready. Deep-fry for 2–3 minutes until golden brown all over, then remove from the oil and drain on kitchen paper.

Wild mushroom fettuccine

We have started a tradition... every New Year for the past three years all our friends pack up the cars and head off to the most beautiful gîte in Normandy. There is a massive kitchen with a huge table that all our families can fit around, log fires and a giant play barn for the kids, who go off and make up plays for us to watch. All we do is eat and drink wine! Jason, my best friend Angela's husband, and I are happy to spend the whole time in the kitchen, either cooking together or taking it in turns. One New Year's Day we made this pasta dish.

Serves 2

30 g (generous 1 oz) dried porcini mushrooms

500 ml (17 fl oz) boiling water

100 g (3½ oz) mini portabello mushrooms

100 g (3½ oz) wild or oyster mushrooms (use your favourite varieties)

150 g (5 oz) fettuccine

olive oil, for frying

2 garlic cloves, finely chopped

150 ml (¼ pint) double cream

truffle oil, to taste

salt and freshly ground black pepper

Cover the porcini mushrooms with the boiling water and leave for at least 20 minutes to soften and puff up. Chop the portobello and wild or oyster mushrooms.

Bring a large saucepan of salted water to the boil and cook the fettuccine until al dente following the instructions on the packet.

While the pasta is cooking, heat a frying pan with a little olive oil, add the garlic and then the chopped mushrooms. Add the soaked porcini mushrooms and the mushroom stock water. Simmer and reduce for about 15 minutes.

Add the cream and simmer and reduce again until the sauce thickens. Season and stir through a few drops of truffle oil.

Mix the sauce and the pasta together and serve immediately.

My two nieces said they didn't like mushrooms and that they wouldn't eat it. However, after a little cajoling (bribery!) we got them to try it... guess what... they loved it!

Mackerel with smoked beetroot
& horseradish crème fraîche

I came up with this dish on *Celebrity MasterChef*. I was cooking for some very special Olympic athletes and I was given the fish course. I wanted to do something slightly different and decided instead of smoking the mackerel to smoke the beetroot. You can buy a smoker for not much money from most good cook shops, and I smoked it in tea. But if you can't be bothered with the faff (my sister will be reading this thinking 'Who has the time?'!) then just don't smoke it. It will produce a different taste, but will still be yummy!

Serves 4

2 fresh mackerel, weighing about 350 g (11½ oz) each, filleted and pin-boned

1 tablespoon olive oil

salt and freshly ground black pepper

1 punnet of micro beetroot, to finish

For the beetroot

500 g (1 lb) small raw beetroot

3 tablespoons basmati rice

2 teaspoons earl grey tea leaves

1 teaspoon demerara sugar

1 tablespoon olive oil

For the crème fraîche

150 ml (¼ pint) crème fraîche

1 heaped teaspoon grated horseradish

a squeeze of lemon juice

To cook the beetroot, preheat the oven to 180°C (350°F), gas mark 4. Wrap the beetroot tightly in foil, place on a baking tray and roast for 1 hour (or longer if the beetroot are quite big). Prick the beetroot with a sharp knife – if it goes in easily, the beetroot is ready. Leave the beetroot to cool slightly and then, wearing rubber gloves, trim off the ends, peel and slice thickly.

To smoke the beetroot, place a sheet of foil in the base of a smoker (or a wok with a lid) and put the rice, tea leaves and sugar in the middle of the foil. Place a rack on top, cover with a lid and place over a high heat. Turn on the extractor fan and open a window. Leave the smoker or wok for about 6 minutes or until it is smoking well. Brush the beetroot slices with olive oil, take the lid off the smoker or wok and put the beetroot in a single layer on the rack – you may need to do this in batches. Cover with the lid again and smoke for 8 minutes. Keep the beetroot warm between batches.

To make the horseradish crème fraîche, mix together all the ingredients and season to taste. Set aside until needed.

To cook the mackerel, score the skin, brush with olive oil and season well. Heat a large frying pan until hot, then add the mackerel, skin side down, and fry for 3 minutes. Turn over and take the pan off the heat – the residual heat will cook the fish.

To serve, divide the smoked beetroot between 4 serving plates. Slice the mackerel fillets in half and lay 2 halves on each plate. Place a dollop of horseradish crème fraîche on top and scatter with the micro beetroot.

Smoked haddock chowder

This recipe started off as smoked haddock with mashed potatoes and peas, a staple in our house to build us up after we had been sick! The trouble is when Billie has been poorly in the past I've made it and she has not been that keen. What she does like though is a soup, so I wanted to come up with something that she would always remember as her 'build-you-up-food' that she will pass on to her family. I've added prawns because she loves them and they add a pretty bit of colour. So, I have taken my memories and reworked them: it's now Billie's 'make-you-better' soup! The result is a hearty, delicious, sweet and creamy soup that will give you a lift on any day.

Serves 4

2 large potatoes, peeled

450 g (14½ oz) undyed smoked haddock fillets, skin on

1 bay leaf

1 shallot, cut in half at the root

600 ml (1 pint) milk

25 g (1 oz) unsalted butter

1 onion, chopped

1 garlic clove, finely sliced

150 g (5 oz) frozen sweetcorn

a handful of runner beans, roughly chopped

150 g (5 oz) raw peeled king prawns

1 tablespoon freshly chopped flat-leaf parsley

salt and freshly ground black pepper

Put the potatoes in a saucepan of water, bring to the boil and then simmer for 15–20 minutes until tender. When cooked and cooled enough to handle, cut the potatoes into small pieces.

Place the haddock, skin side up, in a saucepan with the bay leaf and shallot and cover with the milk. Bring to a simmer for 2–3 minutes and then take off the heat. Leave the fish in the milk to poach.

In a large saucepan, melt the butter over a moderate heat and fry the onion until softened, about 3–4 minutes. Add the garlic, potatoes, sweetcorn and runner beans and stir through.

Lift the haddock out of the milk, peel away the skin and tear the fish into pieces (checking for bones as you do so).

Pass the milk through a sieve into the onion and potato mixture and continue to simmer for about 20 minutes.

Add the flaked haddock and the prawns and cook until heated through and the prawns have turned pink. Stir in the parsley and season. Ladle into bowls and serve immediately.

My MasterChef fish stew

To get into the semi-finals of *Celebrity MasterChef*, I had to think about doing something that really stretched me, but played to my main strength – my palate. I must admit, before the programme I hadn't really ever cooked fish because I was scared I'd make a mistake. Now I'm making up for lost time and this is a staple dish in our household.

Serves 4

15 saffron threads

2 tablespoons olive oil

1 red onion, finely chopped

3 garlic cloves, 2 finely chopped and 1 halved

1 fennel bulb, chopped

1 dried red chilli, finely chopped

1 rosemary sprig, finely chopped

1 bay leaf

1 tablespoon sherry vinegar

125 ml (4 fl oz) dry white wine

1 x 400 g tin chopped tomatoes

50 g (2 oz) ground almonds

1 x monkfish fillet, weighing about 250 g (8 oz), skinned, boneless and cut into chunks

1 x salmon fillet, weighing about 250 g (8 oz), skinned, boneless and cut into chunks

12 whole clams (optional)

4 thick slices of sourdough bread

salt and freshly ground white pepper

For the aioli

2 large egg yolks

2 garlic cloves, crushed

4 teaspoons lemon juice

200 ml (7 fl oz) sunflower oil

100 ml (3½ fl oz) extra virgin olive oil

First, make the aioli. Put the egg yolks, garlic and lemon juice in a food processor or blender with a pinch of salt. Blitz for just 1 minute to combine. Pour both the oils into a jug and, with the processor running, gradually add one-third of the oil through the funnel, until fully incorporated. Slowly increase the stream of oil until all the oil is added and the aioli has thickened. Add more salt and some white pepper to taste. Add a little water to loosen the mixture if necessary. Store in the fridge for up to 1 week if not using straight away.

To make the fish stew, put the saffron in a small jug with 125 ml (4 fl oz) boiling water and set aside to infuse for 15–20 minutes.

Heat the oil in a wide, deep saucepan and add the onion. Cover and cook until softened, about 5 minutes. Add a little salt. Add the chopped garlic, fennel, chilli, rosemary and bay leaf and cook, covered, for about 10 minutes or until the fennel has softened. Then add the vinegar, wine and saffron and its soaking water. Increase the heat and let it bubble for a few minutes. Add the tomatoes and cook gently for 20 minutes.

Add the ground almonds to the pan and adjust the seasoning if necessary. Add the monkfish, salmon and clams, if using. Cook, covered, for 5–6 minutes or until the clams have opened and the fish is cooked. (Discard any clams that stay shut.)

Toast the bread and then rub both sides with the cut sides of the halved garlic clove. Spoon the stew into 4 serving bowls, arranging the fish pieces and clams first and then pour over the sauce. Top each bowl with a piece of garlic toast and add a dessertspoon of aioli on the side or on top.

Lemon sole fillets with brown shrimp butter

There's a great pub near us called The Sun at Northaw that does fantastic food. We started going so much that we became friends with Ollie, the chef, and his wife Sarah who own the place. One of my favourite things to eat there is the lemon sole with the brown shrimp butter; I had to include it in my book. There are two ways to cook the brown shrimp butter – the long, hard way where you take the shrimps, remove the shells and boil the shells with the butter or the easy way, which is definitely the best way for me.

Serves 4

oil or butter, for frying

4 x lemon sole fillets, weighing about 300–400 g (10–13 oz) each

For the brown shrimp butter

100 ml (3½ fl oz) white wine

125 g (4 oz) salted butter

250 g (8 oz) brown peeled shrimps

a good pinch of cayenne pepper

juice of ½ lemon

a handful of freshly chopped parsley (optional)

To serve (optional)

buttered spring greens

red chard tossed in butter and garlic

or a green salad

Gently melt some oil or butter in a heavy-based frying pan and lightly fry the lemon sole fillets for 1–2 minutes on each side until the outside edge turns white. Remove the fish from the pan and keep it warm while you make the butter.

Put the frying pan back on the hob, add the wine and bring to the boil. Add half the butter. When it has melted, add the brown shrimps and the cayenne pepper. Cut the remaining butter into small pieces.

When the butter has boiled with the shrimps and the cayenne it will start to go a little brown. Wait until it smells nutty and goes really brown, this will take about 1 minute, take the pan off the heat and add the rest of the cubed butter and the lemon juice – it will spit so take care at this stage.

Add a little chopped parsley, if using, and then pour the butter over your fish before serving. Serve with buttered spring greens, red chard tossed in butter and garlic or a green salad.

When the butter has boiled with the shrimps and the cayenne it will smell nutty and go really brown

Salmon marinated in soy sauce, coriander & ginger with fennel

We ate a lot of salmon growing up, mainly baked in foil parcels with butter, salt and pepper or poached and eaten cold. When I was a model, I spent a lot of time in Japan. The first time I went was for three months and I was just 17 years old and had a real culture shock – I think I spent my first week in fast-food restaurants! Once I settled down and met a few people I had the time of my life and fell in love with the culture and most importantly, the food! I ate lots of salmon marinated in soy/teriyaki-based sauces and, of course, sushi. This is also lovely as a sauce for salmon sashimi, but just as delicious cooked.

Serves 4

4 x skinless salmon fillets, weighing about 175 g (6 oz) each

2 fennel bulbs

olive oil, for drizzling

For the marinade

4 tablespoons sherry vinegar

2 tablespoons soy sauce

2 tablespoons sesame oil

4 spring onions, sliced

2.5 cm (1 inch) piece of fresh ginger, grated

1 tablespoon freshly chopped chives

1 tablespoon freshly chopped coriander

Put all of the marinade ingredients in a bowl and mix well to combine. Add the salmon, cover and leave to marinate for at least 2 hours in a cool place.

Preheat the oven to 200°C (400°F), gas mark 6.

Slice the fennel lengthways and put the slices in the bottom of a large ovenproof dish. Drizzle with olive oil and bake in the preheated oven for 25 minutes.

Take the dish out of the oven and place the marinated salmon on top of the fennel. Pour over the remaining marinade and return to the oven to cook for a further 10–15 minutes until the salmon is cooked through.

Toria's crispy marinated chicken

My sister, Victoria, is my best friend, my closest family, my constant. When we were growing up we argued loads and had screaming rows but within minutes it was forgotten and we were laughing again. My mum would ask us if we wanted friends round after school, but most of the time we were just happy to play together.

When Mummy died, we became even closer – not just friends now, I think we took it in turns to be the mother to each other. We went out, got drunk, got angry – always knowing we were there for each other.

When I was still running wild, Victoria settled down, met her husband and started her family. I'd never held a baby before my niece Lola was born and when I did I was hooked. My nieces became my world, and Victoria's house became a haven of calm, domestic bliss. I'd turn up unannounced and hungover for cuddles with my girls and home-cooked food, and felt enveloped in love! This chicken recipe was a favourite.

Serves 6

6 x chicken leg portions or 12 thighs, skin on

2 lemons

2 tablespoons freshly chopped tarragon

2 tablespoons olive oil

about 750 g (1½ lb) new potatoes, scrubbed and cut into slices

1 teaspoon paprika

salt and freshly ground black pepper

Preheat the oven to 200°C (400°F), gas mark 6.

Lightly cut the skin of the chicken portions (about 3 times on each). Grate the rind of 1 of the lemons and squeeze the juice from both into a mixing bowl. Add the tarragon, 1 tablespoon of the oil and salt and pepper. Add the chicken and use your hands to coat all the pieces in the marinade.

Put the potato slices in the base of a roasting tin and drizzle over the remaining oil. Arrange the slices, preferably in one layer, but it doesn't matter if they overlap a little bit. Sprinkle with the paprika. Place a wire rack on top of the potatoes and arrange the chicken pieces on the rack. Roast in the preheated oven for 30–40 minutes until the chicken is well browned and cooked through.

Coq au vin

Mummy made this so much when we were growing up, that no recipe exists; it's just in my head. Over the years, I've changed bacon to pancetta and added fresh thyme instead of dried. I don't think carrots are a usual addition to coq au vin, but my mum always put them in, and I have followed suit. She also used quite a bit of butter to brown the chicken – it really does add to the taste and I don't think its worth scrimping on, especially as you're not having it every day. The smell of this cooking immediately transports me back to our family kitchen.

Serves 4–5

8–10 x chicken portions (legs, thighs or a mixture of both)

125 g (4 oz) butter

12–15 shallots, peeled and halved at the root

150 g (5 oz) pancetta, cubed

4 garlic cloves

2–3 sprigs of fresh thyme

10 Chantenay carrots

150 g (5 oz) button mushrooms, halved

1 x 750 ml (1¼ pint) bottle full-bodied red wine

salt and freshly ground black pepper

mashed potato and green vegetables, to serve

Preheat the oven to 160°C (325°F), gas mark 3 and season the chicken pieces.

In a large casserole, melt the butter and brown the chicken pieces. Add the shallots and pancetta and fry for a few minutes. Add the garlic, thyme, carrots and mushrooms and stir well.

Add the wine and bring to the boil. Season, cover and transfer to the preheated oven to cook for about 1½ hours. Trust your instinct here and cook for as long as you like – longer if you like the chicken meat falling off the bone, for example.

Serve with mashed potato and green vegetables.

Rice Krispie chicken

This recipe was my mum's in the days before chicken nuggets. The mayonnaise keeps the chicken beautifully moist and it's always a winner with the kids! Billie loves bashing the cereal and dipping the chicken in the mayo. Be prepared for a mess!

Serves 4

butter, for greasing

250 g (8 oz) Rice Krispies

mayonnaise, for dipping

4 x skinless and boneless chicken breast fillets, weighing about 200 g (7 oz) each, cut into goujons

salt and freshly ground black pepper

potato wedges, to serve (optional)

Preheat the oven to 200°C (400°F), gas mark 6 and lightly grease a baking tray.

Put the cereal and some salt and pepper in a bowl and crumble with your fingers until lightly crushed.

Put the mayonnaise and the seasoned crushed cereal mix in 2 separate shallow bowls ready for dipping.

Dip each piece of chicken first in the mayonnaise, shaking off any excess, before dipping in the crushed cereal.

Place the dipped chicken on the prepared baking tray and bake in the preheated oven for 35 minutes until golden, turning half way through cooking.

Serve with potato wedges, if liked.

John's steak & béarnaise sauce

I'll never forget the best steak I've ever eaten! It was in the backstage kitchen at the Good Food Show Live in Edinburgh. I was with Dhruv Baker (*MasterChef* champ 2010) and the *MasterChef* gang and we were starving. We had just come off stage and John Torode said he would make us a steak. He just seasoned and oiled the steaks, then griddled them. There was some sliced wholemeal bread, no butter, mustard etc., but the steak was cooked SO beautifully it didn't need anything. We ate in silence!

Since *Celebrity MasterChef*, John has become a good friend, someone who I can always ask for cooking help and advice, and who has helped me enormously on this book. His restaurant Smiths do the best steak, chips and béarnaise in London. Here it is!

Serves 4

4 x rump steaks, weighing about 300 g (10 oz) each

a little olive oil

salt and freshly ground black pepper

a bunch of watercress, to serve

For the béarnaise sauce

100 ml (3½ fl oz) white wine vinegar

1 shallot, chopped

a few tarragon sprigs

2 egg yolks

125 g (4 oz) butter, melted

To make the béarnaise sauce, put the vinegar, shallot and tarragon in a saucepan and bring to the boil. Continue to cook until reduced by about three-quarters. Leave to cool and pour into a large stainless steel bowl.

Place the bowl over a pan of just-simmering water – make sure the base of the bowl does not touch the water. Add the yolks and whisk until you can see the whisk leaving a pattern in the sauce.

Take the bowl off the heat and put it on a folded cloth (to keep the heat in) on a worksurface, then start to add the melted butter, little by little, whisking all the time until all the butter is used or your arm has fallen off! Season to taste.

Preheat a griddle pan over high heat. Alternatively, heat a little butter in a heavy frying pan, and preheat the oven to 200°C (400°F), gas mark 6. Season the steaks and rub well with olive oil.

If using the griddle pan, cook the steaks for 3 minutes on each side, to produce medium-rare steaks. Increase or decrease these times by a minute if you prefer your steaks well done or rare respectively. Alternatively, seal the steak quickly on each side in the heavy frying pan and transfer the pan to the oven for 5–10 minutes, depending on how rare you like your meat.

Leave the steaks to rest briefly in a warm place and then serve with a little watercress salad and the béarnaise sauce on the side.

Betty's corned beef pie

I found this recipe in my mum's book. It's handed down from my grandma and I think it must have been a wartime recipe. I asked my dad if he remembered having it – he says he doesn't! I then asked my godmothers who all said it was Mummy's favourite and that Betty used to make it for her. And very vaguely, in the recesses of my mind, I have a memory of eating it cold at the beach hut. I have revived it here, dusted it off and now it's one of my family's favourites.

Serves 6

375 g (12 oz) corned beef, chopped

1–2 onions, grated

50 g (2 oz) Caerphilly cheese, grated

50 g (2 oz) fresh flat-leaf parsley, chopped

a dash of Worcestershire sauce

25 g (1 oz) fresh white breadcrumbs

a drop of milk

1 egg, beaten (optional)

salt and freshly ground black pepper

For the pastry

300 g (10 oz) plain flour, plus extra for dusting

150 g (5 oz) cold butter, cubed, plus extra for greasing

1 tablespoon cold water

a pinch of salt

Preheat the oven to 180°C (350°F), gas mark 4 and grease a 25 cm (10 inch) pie plate or dish.

Make the pastry. Put the flour, butter and salt in a food processor and whizz for about 10 seconds until the mixture resembles fine breadcrumbs. Use the pulse button to avoid over-working the mixture. Add the water and whizz again for 2–3 seconds until the ingredients begin to stick. Collect the mixture together with lightly floured hands and knead lightly on a floured worksurface for 20–30 seconds. Shape the dough into a flat disc. Wrap in cling film and chill for 30 minutes before using.

Combine all of the filling ingredients, except the beaten egg, in a large mixing bowl. Mix until just combined.

Roll the pastry out on a lightly floured worksurface to about 5 mm (¼ inch) thick. Cut out 2 circles from the pastry – one just larger than the pie dish and the other just smaller.

Place the larger circle of pastry in the dish and fill with the corned beef mixture. Top with the second circle of pastry and pinch the edges to seal. Cut a slit in the centre on top to allow the air to circulate. Brush the pastry top with beaten egg, if liked.

Bake in the preheated oven for 45 minutes and serve with your favourite potatoes and greens.

Billie's chive & apple beefburgers

We adopted our beautiful daughter, Billie, when she was 16 months old and our lives changed overnight. Suddenly there was a new little person to look after who had wants and needs and couldn't express herself. She ran everywhere and chatted constantly, but we had no idea what she was saying apart from 'yes', 'no' and 'moo'! I threw myself into being the best mother I could be, making sure she got all the love, cuddles, exercise, fun, stimulation and good healthy food I could give her. From day one she loved these burgers – I think it's probably the apple, which gives them a sweetness – and as she's grown up, she often helps me make them. They are incredibly easy, quick and freeze well.

Serves 4

500 g (1 lb) minced beef

1 apple, peeled and grated (I use Braeburn)

1–2 onions, grated

1 tablespoon freshly chopped chives

a dash of Worcestershire sauce

flour, for dusting

vegetable or sunflower oil, for frying

salt and freshly ground black pepper

To serve

griddled burger buns, salad, onion rings, mayonnaise and homemade Tomato Ketchup (see page 151)

This first step is optional depending on how you like your burgers. Put the mince in a food processor and pulse – this is something I did when Billie was a toddler, simply to make the mince less chewy (I don't do it as much now).

Mix all the ingredients together in a large mixing bowl, season and then shape the mince into either 4 large patties about 5 cm (2 inches) in diameter or 8 mini burgers, which would be ideal for children. Transfer the burgers to the fridge for 30 minutes to chill and then dust with flour.

Heat a little oil in a frying pan and cook the burgers over a medium heat for about 6 minutes on each side until cooked through. Toast the burger buns on a griddle pan, if liked.

Serve the burgers in griddled buns with salad, onion rings, mayonnaise and homemade ketchup.

One day Billie asked to put chives in the burger mix and then proceeded to tell me that they were even more delicious now!

'Perfect Saturday' grilled pork chops & ratatouille

There are very rare moments as a child when you see the bigger picture. You almost look outside yourself and see you in a film, realise what you've got and just how lucky you are. My dad had taken Victoria and me to see *Flash Gordon* at the cinema. We had felt very grown-up going in the late afternoon and we were all chatting about it as we came back home through the front door. The lights were on and the house was tidy and it all seemed really cosy. The smell of pork chops grilling and ratatouille bubbling caused my sister to pipe up 'Mmm, supper smells good!' I remember us all collapsing into laughter. Supper? Victoria had felt it just as I had – that film moment where everything is better than all right with the world – and delivered her line perfectly! We still laugh about it today.

Serves 6

6 x free-range pork chops, weighing about 275 g (9 oz) each

olive oil, for brushing

salt and freshly ground black pepper

For the ratatouille

1 large aubergine

2 tablespoons olive oil

1 red onion, sliced

4 garlic cloves, sliced

2 courgettes, sliced

1 red pepper, deseeded and sliced

1 yellow pepper, deseeded and sliced

6–8 ripe tomatoes, halved

2 fresh thyme sprigs

200 ml (7 fl oz) passata

1 tablespoon balsamic vinegar

4–6 fresh basil leaves, torn

Preheat the oven to 180°C (350°F), gas mark 4.

Slice the aubergine into 1 cm (½ inch) thick slices. Place the slices on a baking tray, brush with a little olive oil and sprinkle over some salt. Bake in the preheated oven for about 10 minutes.

Heat 2 tablespoons olive oil in a large casserole dish and fry the onion until softened, about 5 minutes. Add the garlic, courgettes, red and yellow peppers, tomatoes, roasted aubergines and thyme. Season to taste and stir well to ensure all of the vegetables are browning a little and coated in the olive oil. Add the passata and balsamic vinegar.

Transfer the casserole dish to the preheated oven, turn the heat down to 160°C (325°F), gas mark 3 and bake for 30–40 minutes. Once the ratatouille is cooked, stir through the torn basil leaves.

Meanwhile, preheat the grill. Snip the fat on your pork chops so there are cuts all the way round. Rub them with a little oil and season to taste.

Place the chops under the grill for about 10–12 minutes until cooked through, turning halfway through cooking. Leave the chops to rest for a few minutes before serving with the rich, warming ratatouille.

Mmm, supper smells good!

Angie's lamb mince curry

My mum was an only child and her best friends (my godmothers) were like sisters to her. They are still completely present in my life. My mum taught me by her own example how very important friends are. I have subconsciously mirrored her friendships. The circle continues, and just like Mummy, my girlfriends are like sisters (which also includes my sis!).

Angela, Nicola and I met over 12 years ago and have been best friends ever since. The first night the three of us met we ended up locked in a toilet cubicle chatting until the club had completely cleared out and the cleaners found us! We've been through ups and downs, thick and thin. I have an all-encompassing love for them – they are my daughter's godmothers and I'm theirs. This is Angie's curry: what's lovely about it is that it's got bags of flavour, but it's not too hot so it's family friendly!

Serves 4–6

2 tablespoons vegetable oil

2 large onions, chopped

2 garlic cloves, finely chopped

2 cm (¾ inch) piece of fresh ginger, grated

1 x 400 g tin chopped tomatoes

1 teaspoon turmeric

1 teaspoon cumin seeds

1 teaspoon chilli powder

1 teaspoon ground coriander

1 teaspoon toasted fennel seeds

1 teaspoon toasted coriander seeds

1 whole dried red chilli

500 g (1 lb) minced lamb

100 g (3½ oz) frozen peas

400 ml (14 fl oz) lamb stock

salt

To serve

freshly chopped coriander leaves

natural yogurt

rice or flatbreads

Heat the oil in a large frying pan and add the onions. Cook for 3–4 minutes until softened. Add the garlic, ginger and tomatoes. Continue to cook for 2–3 minutes.

Add the spices and some salt to taste and cook for a further 5–6 minutes.

Add the minced lamb, give it a good old mix and let it cook for 5–10 minutes. Add the peas and stir through.

Add the stock, bring to the boil and let it reduce down for about 20–30 minutes. Remove and discard the red chilli.

Sprinkle with chopped coriander leaves and serve with natural yogurt or a fresh raita, rice or flatbreads.

Angie and Jason live two streets away from me. We are constantly popping into each other's houses, the girls playing together – and we are always eating! The girls love this curry – the little ones who have started the next circle of friendship in this book.

Griddled lamb cutlets
with my mum's mint sauce

My mum used to make this sauce for us to dip our lamb chops into. It was minty and buttery and a little sweet. I asked my dad and my sister if they remembered it and the answer was 'vaguely'. The thing is, it obviously made a real impression on me because I couldn't stop thinking about it. Anyway, I've been trying to work out how she did it, and honestly, it's been driving me mad, I couldn't get it right. This book has so many memories in it and I just couldn't leave this one out... so... I asked my chef friends to help. I was on the verge of giving up when Tony at Smiths handed me a bowl – I dipped my spoon in and as I tasted it I was hit by a tidal wave of memories. Crash! Boom! The tears started falling – this is her sauce.

Serves 3–4

12 x lamb cutlets, French trimmed

oil, for rubbing

salt and freshly ground black pepper

For the mint sauce

100 ml (3½ fl oz) malt vinegar

2 tablespoons freshly chopped mint

3 egg yolks

250 g (8 oz) butter, melted

sugar, to taste

To make the mint sauce, put the vinegar and chopped mint in a saucepan and bring to the boil. Continue to cook until reduced by about three-quarters. Leave to cool and then pour into a large heatproof bowl.

Place the bowl over a pan of just-simmering water, making sure the base of the bowl does not touch the water. Add the egg yolks and whisk until you can see the whisk leaving a pattern in the sauce.

Take the bowl off the heat and put it on a folded cloth (to keep the heat in) on a worksurface, then start to add the melted butter, little by little, whisking all the time until all the butter is used. Season with some salt and a little sugar.

Heat a griddle pan over high heat and rub each lamb chop with a little oil and then a good amount of salt and pepper.

Griddle the chops for about 4 minutes on each side. Transfer the chops to a board or warm place and keep them warm while they rest a little – they are better that way, don't ask me why!

Serve the lamb chops with the mint sauce on the side for dipping. There is plenty of sauce here, but that's much better than not having enough or running out!

Roasted leg of spring lamb

Lamb, or rather the smell of roast lamb, will always transport me back to my Nanna's house. Her and Lely (my most wonderful granddad who I miss every day) lived in an old coach house with a little galley kitchen – I still can't believe the amount of cooking that was done in that tiny space! Victoria and I would often spend the night at theirs and we were allowed to do whatever we wanted – we built camps, made houses, played restaurants, painted and cooked! We loved making drop scones, rock cakes and cola floats. On Sunday, my mum and dad would come and pick us up and Nanna would have made the most beautiful leg of lamb and crispy roast potatoes with mint sauce for all the family to enjoy.

Serves 6–8

1 x leg of lamb, weighing about 2.5 kg (5 lb)

1 whole bulb of garlic cloves

vegetable oil, for drizzling

lots of fresh rosemary

salt and freshly ground black pepper

a selection of vegetables and roasted potatoes, to serve

Preheat the oven to 180°C (350°F), gas mark 4.

Cut little slits with a sharp knife in the leg of lamb – about 20 or so all over. Peel the garlic, cut each clove into slices about the size of your thumbnail and stick them in the holes in the lamb. Drizzle with the oil and season well with salt and pepper.

Take little branches of the rosemary and stick these in the holes next to the garlic so the whole leg looks like a porcupine.

Take the garlic skins and all the rosemary trimmings and drop them into the bottom of a large roasting dish. Position the leg of lamb on top and roast in the preheated oven for about 2–2½ hours (for medium), or until cooked to your liking.

Serve with your selection of vegetables and roast potatoes.

Note: To calculate how long to cook your leg of lamb, as a rough guide, it will need about 30 minutes per 450 g (14½ oz).

Take little branches of the rosemary and stick these in the holes next to the garlic so the whole leg looks like a porcupine.

My husband's actually not bad in the kitchen. He likes his garlic and the first time he made me his carbonara I couldn't breathe near anyone for weeks!

Stacks's carbonara

The first thing Stacks ever made me was sausage, mash and gravy. I'd just got off the train from London to Manchester and was ravenous. He answered the door dressed head-to-toe in Adidas with a steaming plate of food in his hand. It was love!

He won't let me go anywhere near the kitchen when he's cooking, and every time I pipe up, 'Can it have a bit less garlic in the carbonara?', he just tells me to 'Shut up!'

Anyway, it's a good recipe, it's easy and it uses cottage cheese and no eggs – strange but it really does work. Feel free to put as much or as little garlic in as you like. I've put in how much I think is enough – however, I can already hear a 'Shut up' coming my way!

Serves 4

300–400 g (10–13 oz) spaghetti (depending on appetites!)

50 g (2 oz) butter

1 large onion, finely chopped

140 g (4½ oz) pancetta, cubed

2 garlic cloves, crushed

500 g (1 lb) cottage cheese

300 ml (½ pint) single cream

a good grating of Parmesan cheese

freshly ground black pepper

Bring a large saucepan of salted water to the boil and cook the spaghetti until al dente following the instructions on the packet.

While the pasta is cooking, heat a large frying pan and melt the butter. Cook the onion until softened, about 5 minutes.

Add the pancetta and the garlic. When softened and browned add the cottage cheese. Keep stirring until the cottage cheese has melted and the mixture has come together. It will look watery at this stage, but don't be alarmed!

Add the cream, keep stirring and reducing until it has thickened to your liking.

Grate in the Parmesan, add a good crack of black pepper and cook until thick and creamy. And in Stacks's words, 'BOOM!'

Stir the sauce into the cooked spaghetti and serve immediately.

Spanish meatballs
with clams, chorizo & squid

I adore Spanish food. One of my favourite places to go on holiday is a little village called Benahavis near Marbella. There is a restaurant there that we go back to again and again – they do the BEST *Gambas Pil Pil* (see page 88) and these beautiful Spanish meatballs, *albóndigas*. I haven't got their exact recipe but with trial and error and a little help from my cheffy friends these are pretty spot on.

Serves 4–6

25 g (1 oz) butter

3 small shallots, diced

2 heaped teaspoons smoked Spanish paprika

3 garlic cloves (2 crushed and 1 sliced)

2 tablespoons dry sherry

50 g (2 oz) fresh white breadcrumbs

300 g (10 oz) minced pork

1 egg yolk

50 ml (2 fl oz) olive oil

300 g (10 oz) chorizo, cut into bite-sized pieces

300 g (10 oz) cleaned squid, scored and cut into pieces

100 ml (3½ fl oz) white wine

300 g (10 oz) tomatoes, chopped and squeezed into a pulp using your fingers

1 red pepper, roasted (or from a jar of roasted peppers) and blitzed in a food processor to a paste

400 g (13 oz) whole clams

a handful of fresh flat-leaf parsley, roughly chopped

extra virgin olive oil, for drizzling

salt and freshly ground black pepper

fresh crusty bread, to serve

Melt the butter in a heavy-based casserole, then soften the shallots for 5 minutes over a gentle heat. Add the paprika and crushed garlic and cook for 1 minute until the paprika becomes fragrant. Splash in the sherry, then pour the whole lot into a bowl with the breadcrumbs. Mix, season and leave to cool.

Add the pork mince and the egg yolk to the bowl, then mix well with a wooden spoon or with your fingers. Shape the mince into about 32 small meatballs.

Wipe the casserole of excess oil, return to the hob over a medium to high heat and add the oil. Fry the meatballs for 5 minutes, just to colour them, then use a slotted spoon to lift them onto a plate.

Add the chorizo and the sliced garlic to the remaining oil in the casserole and heat until they are sizzling. Add the squid and fry to give a little colour.

Pour in the white wine and bring to the boil, scraping the bottom to de-glaze the pan. Stir in the pulped tomatoes and the blitzed roasted red pepper. Bring to the boil, then add the meatballs and the clams to the casserole.

Cover the casserole and cook for 5 minutes until the clam shells open (discard any that stay shut). Sprinkle with the chopped parsley, drizzle with the extra virgin olive oil and serve with crusty bread to mop up the delicious juices.

Mummy's profiteroles

From about the age of seven my birthday pudding of choice was always profiteroles. Victoria and I adored them fresh with cold cream in the middle and hot chocolate sauce over the top, but loved them just as much leftover from a dinner party the morning after. My mum made great batches of these; I remember them lined up along the kitchen worktops on wire racks, waiting to be filled with cream. She would always say how easy they were to make, but I admit until recently (like a few things in this book) I'd never had the courage to try them. When I did it all came back to me... the colour of the 'dough' and the consistency it's meant to be, which I hope I've explained in the method. On a scale of 1–10, easy being 1, I think this is about a 6! Give it a try, I think you'll be surprised.

Makes about 20 profiteroles

360 ml (12½ fl oz) water

90 g (3½ oz) butter

a pinch of salt and a pinch of sugar

110 g (4 oz) plain flour, sifted

3 eggs, beaten

600 ml (1 pint) whipped cream or ice cream, to fill

For the chocolate sauce

100 g (3½ oz) dark chocolate, broken into pieces

3 tablespoons double cream

Preheat the oven to 220°C (425°F), gas mark 7.

Put the water, butter and a pinch each of salt and sugar in a medium saucepan and bring to the boil – make sure the butter is melted before you continue. Add the sifted flour all at once and beat with a wooden spoon until the mixture leaves the sides of the pan. Put the pan back on the heat and cook for 2 minutes until the paste becomes pale. Leave to cool a little for 10–15 minutes.

Add the beaten eggs a little at a time and beat with a wooden spoon until each bit is incorporated fully – it will go glossy, then back to dull. Continue until all of the eggs have been added, the mix is shiny and it just drops off the wooden spoon. Leave to cool.

Spoon the mixture into a piping bag and snip the end to make a 1 cm (½ inch) opening. Pipe small balls onto a dampened baking tray. Bake in the preheated oven for 10 minutes, then lower the temperature to 180°C (350°F), gas mark 4 for a further 20–25 minutes until golden.

To make the chocolate sauce, melt the chocolate with the cream in a bowl set over a saucepan of simmering water. Stir until the chocolate has completely melted and mixed in with the cream.

When the profiteroles are cooked, turn them over and pop them back into the oven and for 2 minutes to dry a little. Slit each profiterole and leave to cool on a wire rack. Serve them filled with whipped cream or ice cream and topped with hot chocolate sauce.

Millionaire's shortbread

I asked my friend Paul for his mum's delicious recipe for these. I know my mum used to do a version from a neighbour's recipe but I couldn't find it and Paul's mum is 'famous' for hers! She did apparently say, 'This was from before it was called Millionaire's shortbread.' As Paul said, it was probably not the 'done thing' to associate your 'caramel fingers' with money in such a brash manner in postwar Newcastle, which is where his (and my) Nanna was brought up! We knew them as 'caramel fingers', too!

Makes 12 fingers

125 g (4 oz) butter or margarine, softened, plus extra for greasing

50 g (2 oz) caster sugar

175 g (6 oz) self-raising flour, sifted

175 g (6 oz) dark or milk chocolate, broken into pieces

For the filling

200 g (7 oz) condensed milk

125 g (4 oz) butter or margarine

125 g (4 oz) caster sugar

2 tablespoons golden syrup

Preheat the oven to 180°C (350°F), gas mark 4 and grease an 18 x 28 cm (7 x 11 inch) Swiss roll tin.

To make the base, cream the butter and sugar together in a mixing bowl until light and fluffy. Fold the flour into the creamed mixture until well mixed. Press the mixture evenly into the base of the prepared tin and bake in the centre of the preheated oven for about 12 minutes until golden.

Meanwhile, make the filling. Place all of the filling ingredients into a saucepan, bring to a gentle boil, then continue to simmer for 5–10 minutes, stirring continuously. You need to stir quite vigorously as little bits of caramel will stick to the pan but should come away easily and dissolve. Once the sugar has dissolved and the mixture has turned a light caramel colour, take the pan off the heat and spread the filling all over the cooked base. Leave to cool.

Melt the chocolate in a bowl set over a saucepan of simmering water, making sure the base of the bowl does not touch the water. Stir until the chocolate is completely melted and then pour over the caramel. Leave to set for 2 hours or until the chocolate is firm. Cut into 12 fingers.

Chocolate & almond torte
with mascarpone ice cream

I have to say I'm quite obsessed with chocolate and almonds, I use them in my cooking all the time. I wanted to make a rich flour-free torte – the kind that I would like to eat in a restaurant or at a dinner party. I added Amaretto because I love it, but you could add Cointreau and make it orangey if you preferred. This is served best, hot or cold, with mascarpone ice cream and a shot of espresso.

Serves 8

300 g (10 oz) butter, cubed

400 g (13 oz) good-quality dark chocolate, broken into pieces

8 eggs, separated

300 g (10 oz) caster sugar

1 teaspoon vanilla extract or 1 vanilla pod, split lengthways

1–2 teaspoons baking powder

200 g (7 oz) ground almonds

For the mascarpone ice cream (makes about 600 ml/1 pint)

300 ml (½ pint) mascarpone

300 ml (½ pint) double cream

100 g (3½ oz) icing sugar

To make the mascarpone ice cream, beat the mascarpone with a whisk until smooth, then gradually whisk in the cream. Sift the icing sugar on top and whisk until smooth. Pour into an ice-cream maker and churn until set. Transfer to a freezerproof container and freeze until needed. If you do not have an ice-cream maker, pour the mixture into a large freezerproof container and seal. Freeze for 1 hour, then remove from the freezer and use a fork to break up the ice crystals around the sides of the container. Repeat this process four to five times until you have a smooth ice cream with no large ice crystals. Remove from the freezer 15 minutes before using to soften.

Meanwhile, make the torte. Preheat the oven to 160°C (325°F), gas mark 3 and line a 24 x 18 cm (9½ x 7 inch) shallow baking tin with greaseproof paper.

Melt the butter and chocolate in a bowl set over a saucepan of simmering water, making sure the base of the bowl does not touch the water.

Beat the egg yolks with three-quarters of the sugar until pale. Add the melted chocolate and butter. Then add either the vanilla extract or scrape the seeds from the split vanilla pod into the bowl and stir through.

Whisk the egg whites with the remaining sugar in a large mixing bowl, either by hand or with a hand-held electric mixer, until it forms soft peaks. Then add the baking powder. Fold the egg whites into the chocolate mix and then fold in the almonds. Stir well. Pour the mixture into the prepared tin and bake in the preheated oven for 45 minutes.

Julie's crème brûlée

On one of the invention tests I did for *Celebrity MasterChef*, I managed to almost make a crème brûlée without even being aware of it! What's funny about that is that my mum made them a lot, but that fact had completely slipped my mind. It was only when I was flicking through her recipe books and saw Crème Brûlée that I remembered the little ramekin dishes being put under the grill and bubbling away. My godmother, Ann, still puts hers under the grill – however, I like a bit of 'kit', so I use a cook's blowtorch. Ann also puts raspberries in the bottom of her crème brûlées... deelish!

Makes 6

600 ml (1 pint) whipping cream

4 egg yolks

75 g (3 oz) caster sugar

1 vanilla pod, split lengthways

Preheat the oven to 150°C (300°F), gas mark 2 and put 6 small ramekin dishes in a roasting tin.

Put the cream in a bowl set over a saucepan of simmering water, making sure the base of the bowl does not touch the water. Heat very gently, for about 5 minutes, until the cream is warm.

Meanwhile, put the egg yolks and 50 g (2 oz) of the caster sugar in a mixing bowl and beat together well. Scrape the vanilla seeds from the split vanilla pod into the bowl and add the warm cream. Stir with a wooden spoon until mixed well.

Pour the mixture into the ramekin dishes. Pour hot water from the kettle into the roasting tin so that it comes halfway up the sides of the dish. Bake them in the preheated oven for 55–60 minutes. Leave to cool, then chill the ramekin dishes for several hours or overnight.

Sprinkle the tops of the ramekin dishes with the remaining caster sugar and place them under a hot grill until the top caramelises. Leave for 5 minutes for the caramel to harden before serving.

Banana ice cream

We had a massive chest freezer in our garage – the sort you could fit a whole person in! It was always pretty full as if we were expecting a war. Whenever we were bored, Victoria and I would go to the freezer to see what we could find. Almost always we would be looking for Mummy's Banana Ice Cream. I have never to this day tasted anyone's banana ice cream that is anywhere near as good as my mum's, and though I've turned my dad's house upside down, and phoned my godmothers, I can't find her recipe anywhere. Luckily, I have a rather brilliant ice-cream maker that cuts out the old-fashioned way my mum made it (cooling it in the fridge, stirring it, transferring to the freezer for an hour, then beating it, then again after another hour!) and lots of friends to try out my versions on. This was the winner – it's still not my mum's, but as near as I can manage.

Makes 1 litre (1¾ pints)

2 eggs

225 g (7½ oz) caster sugar

1 vanilla pod, split lengthways

500 ml (17 fl oz) double cream

3 ripe bananas, mashed

juice of 1 lemon

Beat the eggs in a mixing bowl and add the sugar. Scrape the seeds from the split vanilla pod into the bowl. Whisk together until thoroughly mixed. Add the cream and whisk again.

Combine the mashed bananas with the lemon juice in a bowl and then add it to the cream. Mix thoroughly.

Pour or spoon the mixture into the basin of an ice-cream maker and set it to churn following the manufacturer's instructions – it will do all the hard work for you!

Alternatively, if you don't have an ice-cream maker you can carry on by hand. Transfer the mixture to a large airtight container and seal. Freeze for 1 hour, then remove from the freezer and use a fork to break up the frozen mixture around the sides of the container. Repeat this process 4–5 times until you have a smooth ice cream with no large ice crystals.

Eva-Rose's banana cake

We have always made banana cake in our family – bananas being a fruit that ripen very quickly, we always seem to be left with unattractive brown ones in the fruit bowl! Using them in this recipe means they don't go to waste – in fact the riper the better! This recipe is one that my niece, Eva-Rose, has developed, putting together lots of recipes we have used over the years. It's simple and delicious.

Makes a 1 kg (2 lb) cake

125 g (4 oz) butter or margarine, softened, plus extra for greasing

75 g (3 oz) caster sugar

75 g (3 oz) soft brown sugar

2 eggs, beaten

3 very ripe bananas, mashed

250 g (8 oz) self-raising flour, sifted

1 generous teaspoon honey

1 generous teaspoon maple syrup

Preheat the oven to 180°C (350°F), gas mark 4 and grease 1 kg (2 lb) loaf tin.

Cream the butter and both sugars together in a large mixing bowl until light and fluffy and then mix in the beaten eggs.

Add in the mashed bananas and stir well. Fold in the flour, mix thoroughly and then stir in the honey and maple syrup.

Pour the mixture into the prepared loaf tin and bake in the preheated oven for about 30 minutes. Lower the heat to 150°C (300°F), gas mark 2 and cook for a further 10 minutes until a skewer inserted into the centre comes out clean. Turn the banana cake out onto a wire rack and try to let it cool before you eat it!

Eva-Rose, my beautiful 10-year-old niece, who's a keen cook

Blueberry muffins

I've had this recipe for years. It's a great breakfast alternative. You can substitute the blueberries for raspberries or bananas if you prefer – they both work very well and they're not *too* unhealthy!

Makes 12 large muffins

100 g (3½ oz) Baker's bran

260 g (8½ oz) wholewheat flour

4 teaspoons baking powder

2 teaspoons bicarbonate of soda

a pinch of salt

480 ml (16 fl oz) natural yogurt or buttermilk

2 eggs

100 g (3½ oz) soft brown sugar

3–4 tablespoons canola oil

2 teaspoons vanilla extract

2 tablespoons runny honey

400 g (13 oz) blueberries

Preheat the oven to 190°C (375°F), gas mark 5 and line a 12-hole muffin tin with large paper muffin cases.

Mix the bran, flour, baking powder, bicarbonate of soda and salt together in a large mixing bowl.

Pour the yogurt, eggs, sugar, oil, vanilla extract and honey into a large jug. Whisk until smooth, then make a well in the centre of the flour and pour the mixture in. Mix well and then add the blueberries. Stir together, taking care not to over-mix.

Divide the mixture between the muffin cases and bake in the preheated oven for about 25 minutes until risen and golden.

Portuguese custard tarts

A few years ago a café opened at the top of our road. The owners were Italian and did great pasta and minestrone soup and we used to go up there a lot for lunch. They also sold these *pastéis de nata*. They became my favourite things and while doing IVF I think these little tarts kept me sane... well, saner! I've had a few goes at making these and I think I might finally have got it right here.

Makes 12

butter, for greasing

250 ml (8 fl oz) double cream

150 ml (¼ pint) milk

grated rind of 1 lemon

1 vanilla pod, split lengthways

4 egg yolks

2 tablespoons cornflour

125 g (4 oz) caster sugar

150 g (5 oz) chilled ready-made puff pastry

flour, for dusting

Preheat the oven to 190°C (375°F), gas mark 5 and grease a 12-hole muffin tin.

Put the cream, milk and lemon rind in a saucepan. Scrape the seeds from the split vanilla pod into the saucepan and drop in the empty pod, too. Bring to a simmer, then take off the heat.

Whisk the egg yolks, cornflour and sugar in a mixing bowl until it comes together in a paste. Pass the milk mixture through a fine-mesh sieve into the bowl of egg paste and mix together quickly and thoroughly.

Return it all to the saucepan and heat over a moderate heat until it thickens – do not let it boil.

Roll out the pastry on a lightly floured worksurface as thin as you can manage. Roll it up into a long sausage shape and cut it into 12 discs. Roll out each disc to about 9 cm (3½ inches) in diameter and press them into the holes of the muffin tin.

Prick the bases with a fork and fill with the custard mixture until just over halfway full. Bake in the preheated oven for about 18–20 minutes until browned on top.

At Easter we made little trees, to hang painted Easter eggs on, had egg hunts for eggs left by the Easter Bunny and made simnel cake.

Simnel cake

I remember my mum making Simnel Cake and being intrigued by the meaning of it. We weren't particularly religious, but my mum loved an 'event' that meant food and socialising! Her Simnel Cake has a layer of marzipan baked into the middle and on top of the cake, and around the top are 11 marzipan balls, which represent the 11 true disciples of Jesus. The 12th ball in the middle is Jesus himself. This cake benefits from being made in advance and being fed with brandy for a couple of weeks; however, it can be eaten straight away.

Makes a 23 cm (9 inch) cake

1 kg (2 lb) raisins

175 g (6 oz) glacé cherries, halved

50 g (2 oz) ground almonds

125 g (4 oz) currants

300 g (10 oz) plain flour

1 teaspoon grated nutmeg

½ teaspoon mixed spice

¼ teaspoon ground cinnamon

300 g (10 oz) soft margarine

300 g (10 oz) caster sugar

6 eggs

1–2 tablespoons brandy

melted apricot jam, for glazing

For the marzipan

500 g (1 lb) ground almonds

250 g (8 oz) caster sugar

250 g (8 oz) icing sugar, plus extra for dusting

2 eggs

½ teaspoon almond essence

½ teaspoon vanilla extract

1 teaspoon lemon juice

Preheat the oven to 140°C (275°F), gas mark 1. Line a 23 cm (9 inch) round cake tin with greaseproof paper (top and sides). Put the raisins, cherries, ground almonds and currants in a large mixing bowl. Add the flour, nutmeg, mixed spice, ground cinnamon, margarine and sugar and beat everything together with a hand-held electric mixer or by hand with a wooden spoon.

Add the eggs, beating in one at a time. Add a teaspoon (or 2!) of brandy and mix well. Leave to rest while you make the marzipan.

To make the marzipan, beat all of the ingredients together in a bowl until it comes together in a smooth dough. Wrap in cling film and store in an airtight container until you are ready to assemble your cake.

To assemble the simnel cake, roll out the marzipan on a surface lightly dusted with icing sugar to about 1 cm (½ inch) thick. Cut out 2 circles the same size as the cake tin. Then, with the leftover marzipan, shape 11 little balls about 3 cm (1¼ inches) in diameter and then 1 slightly bigger ball.

Pour half of the cake mixture into the prepared tin and smooth the surface. Top with one of the marzipan discs. Then pour in the rest of the cake mixture. Bake in the preheated oven for about 3 hours. Leave it to cool in the tin, then turn it out onto a wire rack to cool completely.

Brush the top of the cake with apricot jam and cover with the other marzipan disc. Dip the balls in a little of the jam and place them around the cake, finishing with the big one in the middle. Preheat the grill, then put the cake under to just brown the top – keep an eye on it as it will brown quickly (about 1 minute). Alternatively, use a cook's blowtorch.

Summer

Spicy coleslaw

This is a simple recipe that I use all the time – it reminds me of wonderful, noisy weekends when all my friends and family and all our children gather at one of our houses for long, lazy lunches or dinners. It is great served with Glazed Baked Gammon (see page 214) and pease pudding (or anything, actually).

Serves 8 as a side or picnic dish

1 small white cabbage

1 small red cabbage

2 medium carrots

1 large raw beetroot

1 red onion

4–5 radishes

2–3 tablespoons mayonnaise

juice of ½ lemon

2 fresh red chillies, deseeded and finely chopped

salt and freshly ground black pepper

Grate both cabbages, the carrots, beetroot, onion and radishes into a large mixing bowl. Add the mayonnaise, lemon juice, chillies and salt and pepper and stir well.

Cover and chill until needed, but it is best eaten the same day.

The chilli gives a kick to the usual coleslaw flavour

Sausage rolls

What is it about summers as a child? In my imagination they were boiling hot and sunny and went on forever... but we live in England! The thing is, whenever I talk to anyone about it, they either have the same vivid imagination as me or summers really were beautiful once upon a time. In those heady days there was also no crime or 'bad' people... my sister and I and our two cousins used to go off on our bikes in the morning with a packed lunch in our bags and be gone exploring practically all day. We would lie in the grass making up spy stories and secret clubs, drinking squash and eating homemade sausage rolls.

Makes 10

25 g (1 oz) unsalted butter, plus extra for greasing

2 shallots, finely chopped

2 garlic cloves, finely chopped

2 sage leaves, finely chopped

3–4 fresh thyme sprigs, leaves only

450 g (14½ oz) sausagemeat

1 x 375 g packet chilled ready-rolled puff pastry

flour, for dusting

1 egg, beaten

salt and freshly ground black pepper

Preheat the oven to 180°C (350°F), gas mark 4 and grease a baking tray.

In a frying pan, melt the butter and sweat the shallots and garlic gently for about 5 minutes until they are translucent and softened. Add the chopped sage and thyme leaves, stir through and take the pan off the heat.

Put the sausagemeat in a mixing bowl and add in the cooked shallot mixture. Mix together with a wooden spoon or your hands until thoroughly combined. Season to taste.

Lay the pastry out on a lightly floured worksurface and cut the pastry sheet in half lengthways. Roll half of the sausage mixture into a long sausage shape and place it down the centre of one of the pastry rectangles. Brush the edges with the beaten egg and fold the pastry over the sausagemeat. Press gently to seal.

Repeat with the remaining sausagemeat and pastry rectangle. Cut into 5 sausage rolls each.

Put the sausage rolls on the greased baking tray and brush the tops with the egg. Bake for about 25–30 minutes until slightly puffed and golden brown.

I think you get the gist by now that my mum loved entertaining. She also didn't like staying in! We were always off somewhere and summers were filled with picnics at different places.

Scotch eggs

My mum was really into the Royal Family and I remember us all going to watch Prince Charles play polo (I actually think it was because she was a little bit obsessed with Lady Diana and just wanted to catch a glimpse of her). (The royal wedding was a whole other story!) My mum loved any excuse to make a big picnic with quiche, sandwiches, salads and scotch eggs. I admit that I've added to her recipe – I put in more herbs than she did and some mustard, but the way of making them is the same.

Makes 6

25 g (1 oz) unsalted butter

2 shallots, finely chopped

2 garlic cloves, crushed

a pinch of cayenne pepper

1 tablespoon freshly snipped chives

1 tablespoon freshly chopped flat-leaf parsley

500 g (1 lb) sausagemeat

1 tablespoon Dijon mustard

6 eggs

flour, for rolling

2 eggs, beaten and mixed with 50 ml (2 fl oz) milk

150 g (5 oz) dried breadcrumbs

vegetable or sunflower oil, for deep-frying

salt and freshly ground black pepper

Melt the butter in a frying pan and fry the shallots and garlic until softened, about 5 minutes. Add the cayenne pepper, chives and parsley and stir through. Mix the fried shallot mixture with the sausagemeat in a mixing bowl, add the mustard and season.

Soft-boil the eggs by gently placing them in a pan of boiling water and cooking them for 6 minutes. Cool them in bowl of cold water and then peel them under the water so as not to break the yolks.

Use your hands to shape 6 balls out of the sausagemeat mixture. Place a sheet of cling film on a board, put a ball of sausagemeat on top then another layer of cling film over the ball. Use a rolling pin to roll and flatten each ball in turn so that it is large enough to be wrapped around an egg.

Peel off the cling film and place one soft-boiled egg in the centre of each rolled out sausagemeat circle. Use your hands to wrap and mould the sausagemeat around the egg so that it is completely covered.

Put the flour, egg mixture and breadcrumbs in 3 separate shallow bowls. Roll each coated egg in the flour, then the egg mixture, then the breadcrumbs. Dip in the egg again and finish with another layer of breadcrumbs. Transfer to the fridge for about 20–30 minutes. Preheat the oven to 190°C (375°F), gas mark 5.

Heat the oil to about 180°C (350°F). To test that the oil is ready, drop a cube of bread into the oil and if it turns golden after 20–30 seconds then the oil is ready. Deep-fry the scotch eggs for 2 minutes. Use a slotted spoon to take the eggs out of the oil and transfer onto a baking tray. Bake in the oven for 7 minutes.

Crab dip

Every year we used go to Henley Regatta. This all sounds very posh, but I think my mother had slight delusions of grandeur! We didn't really get involved with the boat racing (until we were a bit older and Victoria's school were rowing and we discovered the boys in their boater hats!), it was all about the food. It always seemed to be a glorious summer's day; all my godmothers would come with their families en masse. We all dressed up for British summertime: sundresses and boater hats. The men would go on ahead of the girls, find a 'pitch', park and set up the trestle tables, chairs etc. Then, the girls would drive down, cars laden with food, wine and kids. Corks would be popped and the tables laid beautifully with cloths and ice buckets and doilies. I have found a few of my mum's lists (written on the back of receipts) of what to cook and bring and they are so precious to me. This was no ordinary picnic – this was a full-on feast! Pavlova (see page 125), Profiteroles (see page 55), Coronation Chicken (see opposite), smoked salmon and Crab Dip. We ate like kings! All the grown-ups drinking and laughing and all the kids running around making camps under the table and paddling in the River Thames. It never did us any harm!

Serves 4–6

250 g (8 oz) cream cheese

2 tablespoons dry sherry

1 teaspoon lemon juice

3 shakes of Tabasco

1 teaspoon dry or wholegrain mustard

1 spring onion, chopped, or 1 small piece of ordinary onion, chopped

white meat from 1 medium fresh crab

1 tablespoon mayonnaise

Melba toasts or crusty bread, to serve

Preheat the oven to 160°C (325°F), gas mark 3.

Mix all of the ingredients together in a mixing bowl. Spoon into a small ovenproof dish and bake in the preheated oven for 15 minutes to warm through and brown on top.

Delicious served warm or cold with Melba toasts or crusty bread.

Coronation chicken

It's funny, as I write this, Prince William is about to marry Kate Middleton and royal wedding fever is everywhere! I am really excited about having a party, not because I'm a staunch royalist, but because I have such fond memories of Princess Diana getting married way back in 1981. I think I've said how much my mum loved Diana, and so the day of the royal wedding dawned sunny and warm and a great big Union Jack flag was hung outside our house. We had a big party with all the usual suspects turning up. I remember catching some of my mum's excitement and thinking how truly like a princess Diana looked in her great big wedding dress. Outside, our back garden was decorated with bunting and a great big trestle table was laid with the best china and a huge array of food – one of the dishes on that groaning table being Coronation Chicken.

Serves 6

25 g (1 oz) butter

1 onion, finely chopped

1–2 teaspoons curry powder

75 g (3 oz) dried apricots, chopped

2 tablespoons tomato purée

600 ml (1 pint) chicken stock

150 ml (¼ pint) double cream

150 ml (¼ pint) mayonnaise

1 tablespoon Greek yogurt

1–1.25 kg (2–2½ lb) cooked chicken, cut into chunks

salt and freshly ground black pepper

½ cucumber, sliced, to finish

Melt the butter in a frying pan and fry the onion until softened, about 5 minutes. Stir in the curry powder and cook for 1 minute.

Add the apricots, tomato purée and stock and bring to the boil. Simmer gently until the sauce becomes thick and most of the liquid has evaporated (about 30 minutes).

Leave the sauce to cool, then stir in the cream, mayonnaise and yogurt and season to taste.

Add the chunks of chicken and stir until well mixed. Serve with sliced cucumber.

Gazpacho

When I taste this I am transported back to Paris in the summer of 1993. I was shooting a film called *Le Peril Jeune*. I was the only English girl and I had been invited over to meet the rest of the cast at the lead actor's apartment. His name was Romain. He was 19 years old, very cocky, funny, beautiful and super-talented – I have to say I fell a little bit in love with him! We spent the whole summer filming, going out partying and hanging around Paris, smoking, him teaching me *verlant* (French slang) and listening to Bob Marley, Cat Stevens and Miles Davis. He made this gazpacho that first night, and I will always remember it – so much so that I managed to track down Romain and ask him for the recipe! He was very happy to send it, and that's how it ended up here. In the words of Romain that summer... *quelle histoire!*

Serves 8

40 g (1½ oz) white bread, crusts removed

500 ml (17 fl oz) iced water

2 garlic cloves, chopped

50 g (2 oz) onion, diced

400 g (13 oz) mixed red, green and yellow peppers, deseeded and diced

400 g (13 oz) tomatoes, skinned, deseeded and cut into quarters

300 g (10 oz) cucumber, peeled and diced

juice of ½ lemon

2 tablespoons olive oil, plus extra for drizzling

500 ml (17 fl oz) tomato juice

1 teaspoon salt

To finish (optional)

150 g (5 oz) mixed red, yellow and green peppers, deseeded and finely chopped

75 g (3 oz) Spanish onion, chopped

Immerse the bread in the iced water and let it soak up the water. Transfer the bread to a food processor or blender and add in the garlic and onion. Blitz until it is a smooth purée. Set aside in a separate bowl.

Put the peppers, tomatoes and cucumber into the food processor or blender and blitz until smooth.

Pour the blitzed tomato mixture into a large bowl and add the lemon juice and olive oil. Also add the onion purée, tomato juice and salt and mix well. Cover and chill in the fridge overnight or for as long as possible (2 hours is really the minimum time).

When ready to serve, check the thickness of the soup and if you need to loosen it add some iced-cold water. Top with some mixed chopped peppers and onion or a selection of garnishes of your choice and a drizzle of olive oil.

Watercress soup

This was a favourite of Mummy's. It always reminds me of our garden at home, laughing with Victoria, swinging on our rickety swing seat, playing with our dolls, while my dad cut the grass and my mum called us in for lunch...

Serves 4–6

25 g (1 oz) butter

1 onion, chopped

2 potatoes, peeled and cut into small cubes

250 g (8 oz) watercress

600 ml (1 pint) chicken stock

2 tablespoons single cream

salt and freshly ground black pepper

Melt the butter in a saucepan and sauté the onion and potatoes for 10 minutes until softened.

Chop the watercress, add it to the saucepan and season. Add the stock, bring to the boil and cook for about 30–45 minutes until the potatoes are tender.

Transfer the soup to a food processor or blender and blitz until you have a smooth consistency. Return the soup to the pan, add the cream and stir through. Ladle into serving bowls and serve immediately.

It always reminds me of English summers in our garden

Cod wrapped in Parma ham
with tomato & olive sauce

I think unless it is deep-fried, cod doesn't have a lot of flavour, so I've wrapped it in Parma ham and made a delicious, sweet, but quite tart, sauce to go with it. Very light and perfect for a summer evening with a lovely cold glass of white wine.

Serves 4

4 x cod loin pieces, weighing about 150–200 g (5–7 oz) each

8 Parma ham slices

a squeeze of lemon juice

salt and freshly ground black pepper

oil, for frying

For the sauce

1 tablespoon olive oil

1 onion, chopped

2 garlic cloves, crushed

1 tablespoon red wine vinegar

1 teaspoon sugar

1 x 400 g tin chopped tomatoes

2 teaspoons capers, roughly chopped

a handful of black olives, pitted and halved

2 tablespoons freshly chopped flat-leaf parsley

Preheat the oven to 180°C (350°F), gas mark 4.

To make the sauce, heat the oil in a frying pan and fry the onion over a gentle heat for 5 minutes. Add the garlic and stir through. Add the red wine vinegar, sugar, tomatoes, capers, olives and some salt and pepper. Bring to the boil and then simmer for about 20 minutes. Stir through the parsley.

Season the cod loins well and wrap 2 pieces of Parma ham around each loin.

Put a griddle pan over a high heat with a little oil and brown the outside of your cod (about 2–3 minutes on each side). Add a squeeze of lemon juice over the top of the fish while it's cooking.

Transfer the fish to a baking tray or ovenproof dish and bake in the preheated oven for about 4–5 minutes until cooked through. Take out of the oven and leave to rest for a few minutes.

Take the oil from the griddle pan and add it to the sauce before spooning over the cod and serving.

Seafood linguine

I think that I started falling back in love with cooking when I hit 30. I was still going out most nights of the week, but there was a niggling feeling of wanting to settle a bit, to make a home, to start making dinners instead of constantly eating out. This was one of my first 'grown-up' dinner party dishes. One night Ange decided to make this seafood pasta but could only find crab. The result, for some unknown reason, was not good and we ended up playing drinking games and taking bets on who could eat the biggest mouthful! After that we stuck to the lobster!

Serves 4

1 tablespoon olive oil

2 garlic cloves, chopped

1 fresh red chilli, deseeded and finely chopped

1 glass of white wine, about 150 ml (¼ pint)

400 g (13 oz) cherry tomatoes or 1 x 400 g tin cherry tomatoes

250 g (8 oz) linguine

1 teaspoon sugar

1 medium cooked lobster

225 g (7½ oz) raw peeled prawns

150 g (5 oz) raw scallops

a bunch of fresh basil leaves, torn

salt and freshly ground black pepper

Heat the oil in a frying pan and fry the garlic for 1–2 minutes until softened.

Add the chilli and stir through and then pour in the white wine. Bring to the boil and continue to boil until it has reduced by half.

Add the whole cherry tomatoes and simmer for 20 minutes, then crush the tomatoes down with a potato masher.

Bring a large saucepan of salted water to the boil and cook the linguine until al dente following the instructions on the packet.

Add the sugar and the seafood and cook until the prawns have turned pink and the lobster and scallops are heated through (only a few minutes).

Stir through most of the torn basil leaves, leaving some for the garnish, and season to taste.

Drain the linguine, but leave a little of the pasta water in the saucepan to loosen the sauce with if necessary. Put the cooked linguine into the pan with the sauce and stir. Place in serving bowls and finish with extra basil and some freshly ground black pepper to serve.

Gambas pil pil

These remind me of our hot summers in Benahavis, pre Billie, sunbathing all day and sitting on the terrace in our favourite restaurant in the evenings, eating these prawns and drinking gallons of rioja... heaven!

Serves 4 as a starter or 2 as a main dish

2 tablespoons olive oil

3 garlic cloves, thinly sliced

1 fresh red chilli, finely sliced

1 teaspoon paprika

250 g (8 oz) raw king prawns in their shells

juice of ½ lemon

1 tablespoon freshly chopped parsley

salt and freshly ground black pepper

lemon wedges and fresh crusty bread, to serve

Heat the oil in a frying pan and fry the garlic, chilli and paprika for just under 1 minute or until the garlic starts to brown.

Add the prawns and cook for 2–3 minutes until they have turned pink. Squeeze over the lemon juice, add the parsley and season.

Serve with extra lemon wedges and crusty bread to mop up all the deeelicious juices!

Hot-smoked salmon fishcakes
with watercress sauce

These fishcakes were one of my dad's favourite dinners from Mummy's summer repertoire. They are a lovely light, summer recipe and one that I always think looks like you've spent ages in the kitchen, when they're actually really simple!

Serves 8 as a starter or 4 as a main dish

600 g (1 lb 2 oz) potatoes, peeled and chopped

400 g (13 oz) lightly smoked salmon fillets

25 g (1 oz) butter

1 tablespoon freshly snipped chives

flour, for rolling

2 eggs, beaten

100 g (3½ oz) breadcrumbs (fresh or dried)

vegetable or sunflower oil, for deep-frying

salt and freshly ground black pepper

salad, to serve

For the sauce

25 g (1 oz) butter

1 shallot, finely chopped

125 ml (4 fl oz) white wine

125 ml (4 fl oz) chicken stock

200 ml (7 fl oz) double cream

100 g (3½ oz) watercress

juice of 1 lemon

Preheat the oven to 180°C (350°F), gas mark 4.

Place the potatoes in a saucepan of water, bring to the boil and simmer for 15–20 minutes until tender.

Meanwhile, place the salmon fillets on a large sheet of foil, dot with butter and wrap the foil over the top so that they are completely enclosed. Bake in the preheated oven for about 15–18 minutes until cooked through.

Drain and mash the potatoes, using the butter from the foil-wrapped salmon. Flake the salmon into the potatoes and mix in – try to keep the salmon chunky. Add the chives and season, then shape into 8 balls (or you could shape into patties).

Put the flour, egg and breadcrumbs in 3 separate shallow bowls. Roll each fishcake in the flour, then the egg, then the breadcrumbs. Dip in the egg again and finish with another layer of breadcrumbs. Transfer to the fridge for about 20–30 minutes.

Heat the oil to about 180°C (350°F) – to test that the oil is ready, drop a cube of bread into the oil and if it floats and sizzles, turning golden brown after 20–30 seconds, then the oil is ready. Deep-fry the fish balls for about 5 minutes until golden. (If you are using patties, fry in a little oil for about 6 minutes on each side.)

To make the sauce, melt the butter in a frying pan and fry the shallot until softened. Add the wine, chicken stock and cream and boil to reduce the liquid by half.

Blanch the watercress, squeeze out the water and blitz in a food processor or blender until it is just broken up. Stir into the sauce and then add the lemon juice, salt and pepper.

Serve with the fishcakes or patties and salad.

Whole trout with lemon, garlic & fennel seeds

We spent many summer family holidays in Spain. One of the things my dad used to do was wake us up really early and take Victoria and I to the fish market in the little fishing village of Moraira – we were fascinated by all the fish. I remember how all the fishermen would sail up to the covered harbour and put their catch on the cool, shaded stone... huge squid, mountains of sardines, great flat fish. Sometimes we would just look and listen to the loud ladies bargaining away in their very fast Spanish, but other times we would buy a fish and my mum would cook it stuffed with lemons and garlic and we would wolf it down, excited that we had seen the journey it had made from sea to boat to market to plate! I can't remember which fish we used to buy, but I am using trout for this recipe.

Great with lemon mayonnaise, or maybe aioli or something like that. Actually delicious if you take the fish off the bone and serve the whole as a lovely salad with crisp baby gem.

Serves 4

250 g (8 oz) baby leeks

1 yellow courgette

1 red pepper, deseeded

2–3 garlic cloves, 1 peeled and sliced and the others left whole

a handful of cherry tomatoes

2 tablespoons olive oil

2 x whole trout, weighing about 500 g (1 lb) each, gutted

1 lemon, sliced

2 teaspoons roasted fennel seeds

salt and freshly ground black pepper

fresh dill, snipped, to serve

Preheat the oven to 180°C (350°F), gas mark 4.

Chop the leeks, courgette and red pepper into thumb-sized pieces so they all roast in the same amount of time. Put in a big bowl along with the whole garlic cloves and the cherry tomatoes and mix with a little olive oil and some salt and pepper.

Transfer to a baking tray and roast in the preheated oven for about 15 minutes. Take out of the oven, set aside and turn the oven up to 200°C (400°F), gas mark 6.

Fill the cavity of the trout with the sliced lemon, the fennel seeds, the sliced garlic and some salt and pepper.

Sprinkle each trout with some oil and then lay them on top of the roasted vegetables. Place in the oven and roast for 15 minutes until the trout skin is crisp and the fish is cooked through. Sprinkle with some snipped dill before serving.

We would drive up to the little fishing village near the farm we were staying at and pick up crab and lobster to cook that evening. Honestly, it was idyllic and we can't wait to go back.

Barbecued lobster with garlic butter new potatoes & chorizo

I have to admit, I'm not one for camping – however, last year, I discovered 'glamping'! We went to a beautiful place in Cornwall called Feather Down Farms. The tents are more like little canvas houses with wood-burning stoves, proper beds, dining tables and a toilet! There are chickens and cows (it's a working farm) and the kids run feral, in and out of the fields, collecting eggs and rolling around in the grass. Of course we went with Ange and Jason and the kids, and Jason and I did the cooking. It was idyllic and we can't wait to go back.

This recipe is all done on the barbecue and wood-burning stove but can easily be cooked in the oven – just cook in a preheated oven at 200°C (400°F), gas mark 6 for 5–6 minutes.

Serves 4

2 x medium lobsters (either cooked or live), weighing about 700 g (1 lb 6 oz) each

500 g (1 lb) baby new potatoes

1–2 tablespoons olive oil

150 g (5 oz) chorizo, chopped

salt and freshly ground black pepper

crisp, green salad, to serve

For the garlic butter

100 g (3½ oz) butter, softened

2 garlic cloves, chopped

1 tablespoon freshly chopped flat-leaf parsley

If the lobsters aren't already cooked, put them in the freezer for 5–10 minutes, then transfer them to a large saucepan of salted boiling water for about 15 minutes until they turn red.

To make the garlic butter, combine the butter, garlic and parsley in a mixing bowl, season with salt and pepper and set aside until needed.

Par-boil the potatoes in a large saucepan of boiling water until almost cooked, about 15 minutes.

Drain the lobsters and cut them in half lengthways. If using live lobsters, remove the stomach sac and intestinal thread. Spoon over a little of the garlic butter and warm through on a hot barbecue for 7–8 minutes.

Heat the olive oil in a frying pan, add the chorizo and the potatoes (bash these with the back of a spoon as they fry to break them up) and cook for about 5 minutes until browned.

Serve the lobster with more garlic butter and the potatoes and a nice green salad.

Tuna poke *with sesame biscuits*

This book is a little bit like therapy – opening up memories that have been lying asleep for a long time. Obviously you don't get to 39 years old without a bit of a past and a few ex-boyfriends along the way! In 2000 I spent a lot of time in Los Angeles, where my boyfriend (Trey) at the time lived. We went on a lot of road trips and I got to see quite a bit of America. He lived with his Japanese friend, Jun, who was very funny and a brilliant artist. Jun introduced me to poke: it's raw tuna chopped up into little cubes with sliced spring onions and sesame seeds marinated in soy and sake and sesame oil. Trey had a beautiful beach house in Hawaii and we spent Christmas and a few weekends there – what's funny is that the supermarket there had poke, so I think it's actually a Japanese/Hawaiian dish. Wherever it originates from, it's one of my favourites.

Serves 4

3 tablespoons soy sauce

1 tablespoon sesame oil

3 tablespoons mirin

250 g (8 oz) raw tuna, diced

4 spring onions, thinly sliced

1 tablespoon sesame seeds

finely chopped chives, to finish

For the sesame biscuits

150 g (5 oz) icing sugar, sifted

50 g (2 oz) plain flour, sifted

100 g (3½ oz) sesame seeds

2 g (¼ teaspoon) salt

100 g (3½ oz) butter, melted

35 ml (1½ fl oz) orange juice

Mix the soy sauce, sesame oil and mirin together in a small bowl.

Mix the tuna with the spring onions in a separate bowl and sprinkle with the sesame seeds.

Pour over the soy mixture and mix. Cover with cling film and transfer to the fridge to chill for at least 30 minutes and up to 24 hours.

To make the sesame biscuits, preheat the oven to 180°C (350°F), gas mark 4. Mix all of the dry ingredients together and then mix in the butter and gradually add the orange juice, blending until smooth. Place teaspoons of the mixture onto silicone paper on a baking tray, leaving room for them to spread while cooking. Bake in the preheated oven for 3–6 minutes. Remove the paper from the baking tray as soon as they are out of the oven, otherwise they will continue to cook. Leave to cool, then carefully peel the biscuits from the silicone paper.

Spoon the tuna mix into small dishes, such as egg cups, top with some chopped chives and serve immediately with the sesame biscuits.

Monkfish
with butternut squash fondant & sauce vierge

This was my winning dish for *Celebrity MasterChef.* I really wanted to impress John and Gregg, but I also wanted to stay 'true' to what was essentially my cooking: really tasty, good food that looked pretty but was not intimidating! I love monkfish, though I would never have cooked it before *MasterChef,* and I thought a light sauce would go very well with it. The butternut squash fondant was an afterthought because I didn't want to use potato. All the flavours really worked together and I was, and still am, very proud of this dish.

Serves 4

50 g (2 oz) butter

300 g (10 oz) butternut squash, cut into rounds, about 5mm (¼ inch) thick

150 ml (¼ pint) fish stock

175 g (6 oz) French beans

4 wafer-thin pancetta slices

4 x monkfish fillets, weighing about 200 g (7 oz) each, skinned and cut into medallions about 2.5 cm (1 inch) thick

1 tablespoon olive oil

a few fresh basil leaves, to finish

salt and freshly ground black pepper

For the sauce vierge

3 tomatoes on the vine, skinned, deseeded and finely diced

1 garlic clove, finely chopped

2 tablespoons freshly chopped tarragon

2 tablespoons freshly chopped basil

100 ml (3½ fl oz) olive oil

2 teaspoons lemon juice

To make the sauce vierge, mix the tomatoes with the garlic and herbs in bowl, then moisten with olive oil and lemon juice to a consistency of your liking. Season well and set aside until needed.

Preheat the oven to 200°C (400°F), gas mark 6.

Melt the butter in an ovenproof frying pan that is large enough to accommodate the butternut squash snugly. Add the squash, and cook over a high heat for 2 minutes on each side.

Pour in the stock, season with salt and pepper and cook in the oven for 20–25 minutes, or until tender.

Blanch the French beans in a saucepan of salted boiling water for about 3–4 minutes. Drain and refresh under cold running water. Pat dry, then separate into little bundles and wrap each with a slice of pancetta. Secure with a cocktail stick. Place on a baking tray and put in the oven for about 5 minutes, or until the beans are heated through and the pancetta is crispy.

Brush the monkfish with olive oil and season well. Heat a non-stick frying pan and cook the fish for 3–4 minutes on each side, or until cooked through.

Place the butternut squash on serving plates, arrange the monkfish around it and spoon the sauce vierge over and around. Place the beans on one side and finish with fresh basil.

Steak tartare

I made this for one of the Good Food shows. It is my absolute favourite starter, but I think people are often too scared to try it at home. It's all down to your taste – so really feel free to put however much or as little gherkin, shallot, mustard etc. in as you like!

Serves 4

150 g (5 oz) beef tail fillet, chopped

1 tablespoon gherkin, chopped

2 tablespoons shallots, chopped

1 tablespoon capers, chopped

a pinch of freshly chopped flat-leaf parsley

1 egg

1 teaspoon Dijon mustard

1–3 teaspoons Tabasco

1 teaspoon Worcestershire sauce

1 teaspoon tomato ketchup

salt and freshly ground black pepper

Melba toasts, to serve

Mix the chopped beef fillet in a mixing bowl with all of the ingredients and season to taste.

Spoon it into four 5 cm (2 inch) ring moulds on a serving plate.

Remove the moulds and serve with Melba toasts.

Chicken with katsu sauce

This is Billie's absolute favourite dinner. As well as loving eating it, she loves making it too, bashing out the chicken to within an inch of its life! In regards to the sauce, I had a great day trying out different flavours and working out my own version of the well-known katsu.

Serves 4

4 x skinless and boneless chicken breasts, weighing about 200 g (7 oz) each

seasoned flour, for dusting

2 eggs, beaten

75–100 g (3–3½ oz) dried breadcrumbs

vegetable oil, for frying

plain, boiled rice, to serve

For the sauce

1 tablespoon vegetable oil

½ onion, roughly chopped

1 garlic clove, roughly chopped

1 tablespoon turmeric

½ tablespoon curry powder

1 tablespoon tomato ketchup

200 ml (7 fl oz) chicken stock

200 ml (7 fl oz) water

1 teaspoon light soy sauce

2 small apples, peeled and grated

1 teaspoon cornflour mixed with 1 tablespoon cold water

salt and freshly ground black pepper

To make the sauce, heat the oil in a frying pan and fry the onion and garlic until softened and slightly brown. Add the turmeric, curry powder and ketchup and stir through. Add the stock, water, soy sauce and apples, season with salt and pepper and simmer for 20 minutes.

Add the cornflour paste and cook for a further 2 minutes until the sauce has thickened. Blend with a hand blender or process in a food processor or blender until smooth. Set aside until needed.

While the sauce is cooking, wrap the chicken breasts loosely in cling film and flatten with a rolling pin or meat tenderiser.

Put the flour, beaten egg and breadcrumbs in 3 separate shallow bowls. Dust each chicken breast with the seasoned flour, then dip in the egg and then coat in the breadcrumbs.

Heat some oil in a frying pan and fry the chicken over a medium heat for about 6–7 minutes on each side until cooked through.

Reheat the katsu sauce gently and serve with the chicken and some plain, boiled rice.

Chicken breasts stuffed with spinach & ricotta

Through *Celebrity MasterChef* I have made some truly great friends, Dhruv Baker (proper *MasterChef* champ 2010) being one of them. On a sunny Friday afternoon he came over and we pottered around my kitchen trying out a few things and giggling at words like 'pollock' and discussing the many merits of cling film! This is one of the summer dishes we came up with. The stuffing can be made a day in advance and kept in the fridge to firm and infuse, but if you don't have time for that make it on the day but give it an hour in the fridge.

Serves 4

4 x boneless chicken breasts, skin on, weighing about 200 g (7 oz) each

oil, for frying

a fresh thyme sprig

1 garlic clove

salt and freshly ground black pepper

new potato salad, to serve

For the stuffing

2 tablespoons olive oil

2 garlic cloves, finely chopped

65 g (2½ oz) chorizo, chopped into small cubes

200 g (7 oz) spinach

25 g (1 oz) butter

a pinch of nutmeg

a pinch of chilli powder

a pinch of sugar

juice and grated rind of 1 lemon

250 g (8 oz) ricotta

1 tablespoon freshly chopped parsley

To make the stuffing, heat the oil in a large frying pan and fry the garlic and chorizo until the oil starts to come out of the chorizo. Add the spinach, butter, nutmeg, chilli, sugar, lemon rind and juice and continue to fry for about 5 minutes.

Put the ricotta in a mixing bowl and stir in the spinach mixture and the parsley. Season to taste, cover and put in the fridge for 1 hour or overnight to set a little and infuse.

When ready to cook, preheat the oven to 180°C (350°F), gas mark 4. Make a slit lengthways in the chicken breasts to form a pocket and season the skin.

Heat a little oil in a frying pan and add the thyme sprig and whole garlic clove. Fry gently for a few minutes to flavour the oil. Place the chicken breasts, skin side down, in the pan and brown the skin for 2–3 minutes.

When browned, transfer to a baking tray and fill the pockets in the chicken breasts with the spinach mixture (a couple of teaspoons in each).

Pour a little of the oil from the frying pan over the chicken breasts and bake them in the preheated oven for about 15 minutes until cooked through. Rest for a few minutes before serving with a new potato salad.

Chicken marsala

When I knew I was going to write this book, I set out armed with a bowl of my Coronation Chicken (see page 81), salad and French bread to see my godmothers (and Mummy's best friends) Ann, Nina and Pat. I'd primed them before and they came over to my dad's house, arms laden with their recipe books and heads full of memories. All three are fantastic cooks, and even though, in my mind, their dinner parties are firmly rooted in the 1980s, they've moved on, still cooking for each other and sharing recipes. We had a great afternoon swapping stories and reminiscing about Henley, the dinner parties, the holidays, Mummy's fiery temper! I asked them what they remembered as my mum's favourite recipe and they all said Chicken Marsala, so here it is!

Serves 4

50 g (2 oz) butter

4–6 x chicken portions (legs or breasts or both), skin on

150 ml (¼ pint) chicken stock

150 ml (¼ pint) marsala or sherry

600 ml (1 pint) double cream

2–3 tablespoons mushroom ketchup

4 tablespoons Worcestershire sauce

a couple of dashes of Tabasco

2 teaspoons English mustard

1 garlic clove, crushed

Melt the butter in a large, lidded frying pan and fry the chicken pieces until golden brown, about 5 minutes. When browned, put the chicken skin side up and cover with the stock and marsala or sherry. Cover with the lid and let the chicken bubble away gently for about 25–30 minutes. Preheat the oven to 180°C (350°F), gas mark 4.

Meanwhile, whisk the cream in a mixing bowl with the mushroom ketchup, Worcestershire sauce, Tabasco, mustard and garlic for about 2 minutes until thick.

Use a slotted spoon to take the chicken out of the frying pan and put in an ovenproof dish. Continue to boil the liquid in the frying pan until it has reduced and is syrupy. Stir the cream into the reduced sauce and then pour it all over the chicken. Bake the chicken in the preheated oven for a further 20 minutes until cooked through.

Sweet & sticky ribs with cornbread

These ribs can be done in the oven and then finished off on the barbecue. If you can get hickory wood chips stick them on the barbie to get that lovely smoky flavour.

Serves 6

about 2 kg (4 lb) baby back or pork ribs, cut individually

200 ml (7 fl oz) tomato ketchup

200 ml (7 fl oz) orange juice

50 g (2 oz) runny honey

1 tablespoon English mustard

3 tablespoons Worcestershire sauce

3 tablespoons dark, soft muscovado sugar

1 teaspoon cornflour

For the cornbread

125 g (4 oz) self-raising flour

125 g (4 oz) cornmeal

150 g (5 oz) tinned sweetcorn, drained

1 teaspoon baking powder

2 teaspoons sugar

175 ml (6 fl oz) milk

125 g (4 oz) unsalted butter, plus extra for greasing

1 egg, beaten

6 streaky bacon rashers, fried until crispy and cut into lardon strips

salt and freshly ground black pepper

The day before (or while you are barbecuing the ribs if you are doing it all on the barbecue), make the cornbread. Preheat the oven to 190°C (375°F), gas mark 5 and grease a loaf tin or square cake tin. Sift the flour into a large bowl and add the cornmeal, sweetcorn, baking powder and sugar.

Put the milk and butter into a saucepan and cook over a very low heat until the butter has melted. Mix the buttery milk into the flour mixture with the beaten egg until it is well combined. Add half of the bacon strips and some salt and pepper. Pour the mixture into the prepared tin and sprinkle over the rest of the bacon. Bake in the preheated oven for 25 minutes.

When you are ready, begin to prepare the ribs. Preheat the barbecue to low or oven to 120°C (250°F), gas mark ½. In a large shallow dish, combine the tomato ketchup, orange juice, honey, mustard, Worcestershire sauce and muscovado sugar. Add the ribs and turn in the marinade to make sure they are well coated. Cover with cling film and chill for at least 1 hour or as long as possible.

Once marinated, place the ribs either in foil if you're putting them on the barbecue or in a shallow baking tray if baking in the oven. Brush over some of the marinade left in the dish and then cover with foil so that they don't dry out. Barbecue or bake in the preheated oven for 1½ hours until tender.

Turn the heat up to high on the barbecue or to 200°C (400°F), gas mark 6. Unwrap the ribs and pour any of the juices from the pan or foil into a saucepan. Brush the ribs with a little more marinade and cook for 10–15 minutes straight on the barbecue or uncovered on a clean baking tray in the oven until golden and sticky.

Meanwhile, simmer the marinade in the saucepan over a medium heat for 10 minutes. Mix the cornflour with 1 tablespoon cold water and add this to the pan. Cook for 2 minutes. When the ribs are done, brush over the sauce and serve with the cornbread.

Barbecued lamb

This is a lovely summer recipe. We had loads of barbecues when we were younger. As soon as the sun came out my mum would seem instantly brighter, the sunbed would be taken out of the garage and the smell of suntan oil would fill the air!

Serves 6

75 g (3 oz) sun-dried tomatoes, drained and roughly chopped

2–3 garlic cloves, crushed

1 tablespoon freshly chopped mint

grated rind and juice of 1 lemon

½ tablespoon olive oil, plus extra for rubbing

½ tablespoon Dijon mustard

1 x butterflied lamb leg (ask your butcher to do this for you), weighing about 750 g (1½ lb)

salt and freshly ground black pepper

To finish

finely chopped fresh mint

grated rind of 1 lemon

Preheat the barbecue to high if you are using gas or light the barbecue about 45 minutes before cooking if using charcoal – the embers should be glowing with no traces of black coal left.

Mix the sun-dried tomatoes, garlic, mint, lemon rind and juice, oil, mustard and some salt and pepper together in a mixing bowl.

Make cuts about 2 cm (¾ inch) deep in the meat all over and stuff with the tomato mixture. Rub all over with olive oil and more salt and pepper.

Place the lamb on the barbecue for about 12–15 minutes on each side or until cooked to your liking and then leave to rest for 10 minutes. Cut the lamb into slices and then finish with chopped fresh mint and grated lemon rind.

Note: This can also be done in an oven preheated to 180°C (350°F), gas mark 4. Cook for about 45–60 minutes or until cooked to your liking and then rest for 10–15 minutes.

What is it about summers as a child? In our heads they always seemed so long, hot and full of sunshine!

Canon of lamb & salsa verde

Now, this is the Salsa Verde recipe I did on *Celebrity MasterChef* and had to cook on the Orient Express – it was a truly amazing experience! I served it with parsnip purée, but here, because it's summer, I'm serving it with a white and green bean salad.

Serves 4

2 x canons of lamb, weighing about 200 g (7 oz) each

vegetable oil, for rubbing

75 g (3 oz) butter

salt and freshly ground black pepper

For the salsa verde

½ bunch of fresh flat-leaf parsley

2 fresh rosemary sprigs, leaves removed from the stem

½ bunch of fresh mint

½ bunch of fresh basil

about 4–5 small gherkins

2 garlic cloves

1 tablespoon Dijon mustard

6 anchovy fillets

1 tablespoon capers

grated rind of ½ lemon

8 tablespoons extra virgin olive oil

3 tablespoons white wine vinegar

For the white & green bean salad

25 g (1 oz) butter

1 x 410 g tin butter beans, drained

1 x 410 g tin cannellini beans, drained

150 g (5 oz) runner beans, blanched

a squeeze of lemon juice

Preheat the oven to 180°C (350°F), gas mark 4.

To make the salsa verde, put all of the herbs into a food processor or blender and blitz until roughly chopped. Add the gherkins, garlic, mustard, anchovy fillets, capers, lemon rind, oil and vinegar and blitz again.

Take a large ovenproof frying pan and heat it over a high heat. Rub the canons of lamb all over with oil and season really well.

Drop the canons in the hot pan and add a little more oil. After 1–2 minutes turn the canons – you will need to turn a few times to colour the lamb all over. Do this over a high heat and do it quickly, or the lamb will be dry and tough.

Add the butter to the pan, melt and then transfer the pan to the preheated oven and cook for 6 minutes. Take out of the oven and leave to rest for about the same amount of time.

Meanwhile, make the white and green bean salad. Melt the butter in a frying pan and warm through the butter beans and cannellini beans. Stir the runner beans into the white beans, add a good squeeze of lemon and season to taste.

Slice the lamb and serve on the white and green bean salad with the salsa verde.

Pizza

Billie, of course, loves making pizza dough. In fact, she prefers making the pizza to eating it! At Feather Down Farms (see page 96) they have a pizza oven outside the tent and we make pizza for all the kids to devour!

Makes 4–6 medium pizzas

250–350 ml (8–12 fl oz) lukewarm water

1 x 7 g sachet dried yeast

550 g (1 lb 3½ oz) strong white flour, plus extra for dusting

1 teaspoon salt

2 teaspoons caster sugar

2 tablespoons olive oil

For the tomato sauce

1 tablespoon olive oil

1 onion, finely chopped

1 garlic clove, finely chopped

2 x 400 g tins chopped tomatoes

salt and freshly ground black pepper

For the topping (you can put anything you like on – this is just a guide)

100 g (3½ oz) Buffalo mozzarella

a handful of fresh basil leaves

8–10 salami slices

a handful of green olives, pitted

1 yellow pepper, deseeded and sliced

Pour 150 ml (¼ pint) of the water into a bowl and sprinkle over the yeast. Stir to dissolve and then leave to stand in a warm place for 10 minutes (this activates the yeast).

Sift the flour, salt and sugar into a large bowl. Stir the oil into the yeast mixture until well combined.

Make a well in the centre of the dry ingredients and pour in the yeast mixture, mixing to form a soft and slightly sticky dough. Add enough of the remaining water, little by little, until you have achieved the correct consistency.

Transfer the dough to a lightly floured worksurface and lightly flour your hands. Knead the dough for 10 minutes until it is smooth and pliable.

Place the dough into a large bowl and cover with cling film. Set aside in a warm place for 1 hour until it has doubled in size.

Meanwhile, make the tomato sauce. Heat the oil in a frying pan. Cook the onion until softened, about 5 minutes, then add the garlic and cook for a few minutes. Add the tomatoes and bring to the boil. Simmer and reduce the sauce for about 30 minutes.

Remove the proved dough from the bowl and knead it again until smooth. Separate into 4 pieces, then lightly flour the worksurface and shape with your hands to large round pizza shapes about 5 mm (¼ inch) thick. Preheat the oven to 190°C (375°F), gas mark 5.

Place the dough in well-floured pizza tins or on baking trays, top with tomato sauce and your choice of toppings and bake in the preheated oven for 12–15 minutes until crispy.

Note: You can either use the dough immediately, or keep it, wrapped in cling film, in the fridge (or freezer) until required.

Key lime pie

I love this recipe – it's always a good one to make if asked to bring a pudding to a summer dinner party or barbecue. It's fresh and light, and looks very impressive, even though it's actually quite easy to make.

Serves 8–10

125 g (4 oz) butter

250 g (8 oz) digestive biscuits, crushed

lime slices, to finish (optional)

For the filling

3 large egg yolks

finely grated rind of 3 limes

1 x 397 g tin condensed milk

juice of 5 limes

Preheat the oven to 180°C (350°F), gas mark 4.

Melt the butter in a frying pan. Add the crushed biscuits and mix together. Press this mixture into the base of 23 cm (9 inch) flan dish. Bake in the preheated oven for about 10 minutes.

Meanwhile, make the filling. Whisk the egg yolks and lime rind together until the yolks are pale and thick. Whisk in the condensed milk for a further few minutes and then whisk in the lime juice.

Pour the filling mixture onto the cooked biscuit base and return to the oven for a further 15–20 minutes until it is just set. Leave the pie to cool, then cover and refrigerate until you want to eat it. Decorate with slices of lime if liked.

Vanilla cheesecake

Mummy's cheesecake was the lightest I've ever had. I remember going to a restaurant and ordering it because I loved my mum's so much, only to be served a rubbery, soft based, thick, sickly wedge! I looked at my mother in dismay and she told me that was a baked cheesecake, and not a good one! Years later when I spent time in LA I discovered The Cheesecake Factory, a restaurant that did thousands of different kinds of cheesecake. I sampled many, and I know it's all a question of personal taste... but none of them were as good as my mum's.

When I went to write this recipe up it was on a scrap of paper I found in my mums stuff years ago. While collecting all of it together for this book I lost her precious recipe (that'll teach me for never copying it out). I remembered the basic ingredients and I hope that this is as near as dammit to her original.

Serves 6

85 g (3½ oz) butter

1 dessertspoon caster sugar

140 g (4½ oz) digestive biscuits, crushed

fruit, to finish

strong coffee or espresso, to serve

For the filling

475 g (15 oz) cream cheese

160 g (5½ oz) caster sugar

grated rind of 1 lemon

160 ml (5½ fl oz) soured cream

160 ml (5½ fl oz) double cream

a splash of vanilla extract

Melt the butter and the sugar together in a saucepan over a gentle heat and then pour into a bowl containing the crushed biscuits. Mix thoroughly.

Line a 23 cm (9 inch) springform cake tin with greaseproof paper. Spoon the biscuit mixture into the tin and press it down to form a firm, well-packed base. Leave in the fridge to set for about 30 minutes.

Meanwhile, make the filling. Beat the cream cheese in a bowl to soften it and then add half the sugar and the lemon rind. In a separate bowl, mix the soured cream, double cream, the remaining sugar and the vanilla extract together and then whisk until it forms firm peaks – you should be able to turn the bowl over your head and the mixture be firm enough to stay put.

Fold the cream cheese mixture into the cream and then pour it all onto the chilled biscuit base. Chill for at least 4 hours or preferably overnight.

You can top with fruit, if liked, and serve with little cups of strong coffee or espresso.

Fantasy cake

My friend Mary is a fantastic cook! One day we met up for a picnic in the park, she came rushing out of her house with a tiffin tin and picnic blanket, saying how she had just baked this cake and that she hoped it would be OK. When she opened the lid of the tin the most beautiful smell of warm cake and strawberries filled the air. It was still warm and the strawberries deliciously gooey, and I honestly thought I might have died and gone to heaven it was that good! Every time I saw her I would go on about the cake, asking for the recipe and waxing lyrical about how beautiful it was. She said she didn't really have a recipe but that she would email me something – we nicknamed it the 'fantasy' cake! It now happens to be Billie's favourite cake and we make it all the time. Over the years I have adapted it a little, and have tried all sorts of different fruit, such as raspberries, blackberries and other summer berries – use your favourite.

Serves 6–8

175 g (6 oz) unsalted butter, softened, plus extra for greasing

150 g (5 oz) caster sugar

150 g (5 oz) self-raising flour, sifted

2 eggs

3 tablespoons milk

100 g (3½ oz) ground almonds

1 teaspoon almond essence

400 g (13 oz) strawberries, hulled and halved or quartered depending on size, or raspberries, or both

icing sugar, for dusting

Preheat the oven to 160°C (325°F), gas mark 3 and grease and line a 23 cm (9 inch) loose-bottomed cake tin.

Cream the butter and sugar together in a large mixing bowl until light and fluffy. Then add in the flour, eggs, milk, ground almonds and almond essence and mix well. Stir in the fruit, reserving a handful for decorating.

Pour the mixture into the cake tin and put the remaining handful of fruit on top of the cake.

Bake in the preheated oven for about 1–1¼ hours. To test if it is cooked, pierce the cake with a skewer – if it is clean when you pull it out the cake is cooked, if it's not, return the cake for another 5–10 minutes and check again. Careful not to overcook!

Turn the cake out of the tin onto a wire rack to cool and dust with icing sugar. It is best served just as it is turning from warm to room temperature.

Summer berry mille feuille
with vanilla cream

The royal wedding continued... after lunch in the garden we all walked up to the station to wave at the newlyweds as they passed us on the royal train. I don't know if I remember this from the television or that I actually caught a glimpse of Princess Di, but she was wearing pink and looked really happy!

Serves 4

butter, for greasing

200 g (7 oz) chilled ready-rolled puff pastry

2 tablespoons icing sugar, plus extra for dusting

300 g (10 oz) strawberries, hulled and sliced

300 g (10 oz) raspberries, sliced

For the vanilla cream

1 vanilla pod, split lengthways

150 ml (¼ pint) double cream

1 tablespoon icing sugar

Preheat the oven to 190°C (375°F), gas mark 5 and grease a baking tray.

Dust the worksurface and the pastry with icing sugar and cut the pastry into 6 circles or rectangles. Prick all over with a fork, put on the prepared baking tray and bake in the preheated oven for about 15 minutes until golden brown. Leave to cool.

Once the pastry has cooled completely, cut each pastry circle or square horizontally in half, giving you 12 thin halves of pastry (you will need 3 halves for each stack).

To make the vanilla cream, scrape the seeds from the split vanilla pod into the cream in a mixing bowl. Add the icing sugar and whisk until thick.

Put a pastry sheet on a plate, spread with the cream and then top with some berries. Add the next pastry sheet and repeat the layers of cream and berries. Top with a third pastry sheet and dust with icing sugar before serving.

After waving at the train, I remember walking back to our house in the sunshine for cups of tea scones and jam and my favourite Summer Berry Mille Feuille!

My mum's pavlova

There were two best things about my mum's endless stream of dinner parties. The first was that all the kids would always congregate on the stairs, giggling and laughing at the grown-ups' conversation. The second was the leftovers. My sister and I would creep down the stairs and eat whatever escaped being devoured the night before – normally it was still on the dining room table. The best was my mum's pavlova. It was crispy on the outside but deliciously soft and chewy in the middle, topped with strawberries and raspberries on cream. It always looks so impressive, but it's really easy. I promise.

Serves 6

3 egg whites

a pinch of salt

250 g (8 oz) caster sugar

1 teaspoon vanilla extract

1 teaspoon malt vinegar (or any you have to hand)

300 ml (½ pint) double cream

1 x 400 g tin raspberries in syrup or juice (optional)

250 g (8 oz) strawberries, hulled and sliced

250 g (8 oz) raspberries

Preheat the oven to 140°C (275°F), gas mark 1. Draw a 23 cm (9 inch) circle on non-stick baking paper as a guide and place on a baking tray.

Whisk the egg whites with the salt in a large clean bowl, either by hand or with a hand-held electric mixer, until very stiff, then gradually whisk in the sugar. Whisk until it forms stiff peaks, this takes about 3–4 minutes. Fold in the vanilla extract and vinegar.

Spread the meringue mixture over the circle on the non-stick paper and bake in the preheated oven for 1 hour until firm.

Mummy's trick (which I always do and believe is the 'key' to a perfect meringue) was to turn off the oven and leave the meringue in with the door closed for another half an hour.

Leave the meringue to cool and peel off the baking paper from the bottom with care. Place the pavlova on a serving plate.

Whip the cream until stiff, pile on top of the meringue and decorate with the fruit. I strain the tinned raspberries and pile them in the centre, then arrange the rest of the fruit on the top. Of course, you can use whatever fruit is in season.

Scones & really quick raspberry jam

I originally found this jam recipe in a Weight Watchers book I have (I put on a load of weight when I did IVF and Weight Watchers was brilliant and really worked for me). It really is the easiest way of making jam (obviously, it only lasts a few weeks in the fridge and isn't completely jam-like), but if you need a quick fix to go on your scones, it's brilliant.

Makes 16

375 g (12 oz) self-raising flour, plus extra for dusting

1 teaspoon salt

2 teaspoons baking powder

2 tablespoons caster sugar

75 g (3 oz) cold butter, cubed, plus extra for greasing

175 ml (6 fl oz) milk, plus extra for brushing

clotted cream, to serve

For the jam (makes about 350 g /11½ oz)

200 g (7 oz) raspberries

200 g (7 oz) caster sugar

To make the jam, preheat the oven to 180°C (350°F), gas mark 4 and clean and sterilise a jam jar.

Place the raspberries and caster sugar in 2 separate ovenproof dishes. Bake in the preheated oven for 20 minutes. Pour the sugar into the raspberries and mix together well. Pour into the clean jam jar. Leave to cool completely before serving.

To make the scones, preheat the oven to 200°C (400°F), gas mark 6 and grease a baking tray.

Sieve the flour, salt and baking powder together into a mixing bowl and add the sugar and butter and rub together until the mixture resembles breadcrumbs.

Mix in the milk to make a dough, and knead a little until it becomes smooth.

Roll the dough out on a lightly floured surface to about 1 cm (½ inch) thick and cut out about sixteen 5–6 cm (2–2½ inch) rounds. Put the dough circles on the prepared baking tray and brush with a little milk. Bake in the preheated oven for about 10–12 minutes until risen and golden.

Serve the scones with the jam and some clotted cream.

Scones and jam and a cup of tea in the garden, dozing in the shade with the hum of a lawnmower in the background...

Summer pudding

I found this on my mum's list of things to take to one of our picnics at Henley Regatta. How she transported all these things is amazing, but she did, and it stayed cool and was as perfectly refreshing as it should be.

Serves 6–8

butter, for greasing

8 slices of stale, crustless white bread, 1 cm (½ inch) thick

750 g (1½ lb) mixed fruit (see Note)

125 g (4 oz) caster sugar

clotted cream, to serve

Lightly grease a 900 ml (1½ pint) soufflé dish or pudding basin (this helps the bread to stick and helps with the 'un-moulding' at the end), then line with 1 or 2 slices of bread to cover the base completely. Line the sides of the dish with more bread – if necessary, cut the bread to shape to fit closely together.

Hull and carefully wash the fruit (pit cherries, if using). Place the fruit in a heavy-based pan and sprinkle the sugar over. Bring to the boil over a low heat and cook for 2–3 minutes, just until the sugar melts and the juices begin to run.

Take the pan off the heat and set aside 1–2 tablespoons of the fruit juices. Spoon the fruit and remaining juice into the bread-lined dish and cover the surface closely with the rest of the bread.

Put a plate that fits inside the dish on top of the pudding and weight it down with a heavy tin or jar. Transfer the pudding to the fridge to chill for 8 hours.

Before serving, remove the weight and plate. Cover the dish with the serving plate and turn upside down to un-mould the pudding. Use the reserved fruit juice to pour over any parts of the bread that have not been soaked through and coloured by fruit juices. Serve with clotted cream.

Note: Strawberries, raspberries, red and black currants, black pitted cherries are all suitable for this dish and can be mixed according to taste and availability. The more varied the fruit, the tastier the result, but be careful with too many blackcurrants as they tend to dominate.

It's also another one on the list of 'easy but looks impressive!

Autumn

Mummy's French onion soup

This soup will always remind me of Halloween as my mum used to make it for our parties. I think I've said before that when my nieces were born, they changed my life. I suddenly had two little people to care about and buy stuff for, and watch grow up! The minute they were old enough to even vaguely understand Halloween, I got completely overexcited, made them costumes and took them 'trick or treating'. When we came home, freezing cold and starving, Victoria had revived Mummy's French Onion Soup recipe, and so the cycle continues...

Serves 4–6

75 g (3 oz) butter

4 large onions, thinly sliced and pushed out into rings

2 tablespoons plain flour

½ tablespoon salt

½ tablespoon freshly ground black pepper

900 ml (1½ pints) beef stock

6 small circles of French bread cut 1.5 cm (¾ inch) thick

3 garlic cloves, halved

75 g (3 oz) Parmesan cheese, finely grated

In a medium-sized, heavy flame-proof casserole dish, melt the butter over a moderate heat. When the foam subsides, reduce the heat to low and add the onions. Cook, stirring occasionally, for 25–30 minutes, or until golden brown. Take off the heat and with a wooden spoon stir in the flour, salt and pepper. Gradually add the stock, stirring all the time. Return the casserole dish to the heat, turn up to high and bring the soup to the boil. Then reduce the heat again to low, cover the dish and simmer for 20 minutes.

Meanwhile, preheat the grill to high. Rub each circle of bread on each side with a garlic half and place under the grill until very slightly toasted. Discard the garlic.

Take the casserole off the heat, float the toast slices on top of the soup, sprinkle the Parmesan over the toast and place the casserole under the grill for 5 minutes to bubble and brown.

Daddy's soup

My lovely friend Jasee (Angela's husband) makes this in vats all the time for the kids. Whenever we are round at theirs and the kids ask what's for tea, Daddy's Soup gets cheers all round! Billie calls it 'Daddy's Soup', even though it's not her daddy that makes it, and she asks for it so much that if Jasee hasn't sent over a supply of it, I make it under her watchful eye. The biggest compliment I get is when she says, 'Mummy, this is just like Uncle Jasee's.' What's also ace about this soup is that you feel really great that your kids are eating only healthy stuff and loving it at the same time!

Serves 4–6

1 onion

2 carrots, peeled

2 celery sticks

1 parsnip, peeled

1 garlic clove, finely chopped

50 g (2 oz) butter

500 g (1 lb) diced lamb

flour, for dusting

vegetable oil, for frying

500 ml (17 fl oz) vegetable stock

750ml (1¼ pints) passata

½ bag curly kale, about 100 g (3½ oz)

1 x 400 g tin mixed pulses, drained

50 g (2 oz) green beans, chopped into thirds

2 bay leaves

1 fresh rosemary sprig

2 fresh thyme sprigs, leaves only

2 handfuls of macaroni

grated Parmesan cheese, to finish

Chop all the vegetables into 1 cm (½ inch) cubes. Melt the butter in a heavy-based saucepan and sweat the garlic and all of the vegetables until softened.

Dust the lamb in flour. Heat some oil in a separate frying pan and brown the meat – brown in batches if necessary. Add the meat to the vegetables and then pour the stock into the meat pan to deglaze the pan. Transfer this stock to the vegetables along with the passata and cook over a low heat for 1 hour.

Add the kale, pulses, green beans and herbs to the pan and continue to cook for another 30 minutes.

Bring a large saucepan of salted water to the boil and cook the macaroni until al dente following the packet instructions and then add it to the soup.

Serve the soup with some grated Parmesan over the top.

Leek & potato soup

We had great Bonfire Nights! My sister, our cousins and I would make a Guy to put on top of the bonfire my dad had made in the back garden, everyone would turn up and bring a dish and there were sparklers, fireworks and lots of laughter! I remember one Bonfire Night my wonderful grandfather, Lely, sat all the children around the fire and told us ghost stories. We were transfixed – steaming mugs of leek and potato soup in our hands and our imaginations going into overdrive. Needless to say, we didn't sleep for weeks!

Serves 4–6

50 g (2 oz) butter

1 onion, finely chopped

1 garlic clove, crushed

450 g (14½ oz) leeks, sliced

450 g (14½ oz) potatoes, diced into 1 cm (½ inch) cubes

1 litre (1¾ pints) chicken stock

150 ml (¼ pint) double cream

salt and freshly ground black pepper

In a large saucepan, melt the butter over a medium heat. Fry the onion, garlic and leeks until softened and the leeks are just starting to fall apart.

Add the potatoes and cook for a further few minutes. Add the stock, bring to the boil and simmer for about 20 minutes, until the potatoes are tender.

Transfer the soup to a food processor or blender and blitz until smooth. Alternatively, use a hand blender to liquidise the soup.

Season, stir through the cream and check the seasoning again before serving.

Pumpkin & almond soup

When we were away in France last year we went to a little French restaurant that opened on New Year's Day just for us. The chef and his wife owned the restaurant; they spoke no English and kept bringing us out delicious *amuse-bouches* between courses. One of the things they served was a pumpkin soup in small kilner jars. I tried to recreate it as soon as I got home, and this is my version.

Serves 4–6

1 small pumpkin, peeled, deseeded and roughly chopped

1 onion, roughly chopped

2 garlic cloves

1 tablespoon freshly chopped thyme, plus extra for serving

3 tablespoons olive oil

75 g (3 oz) toasted flaked almonds

500 ml (17 fl oz) chicken stock, or use vegetable stock if serving to vegetarians

150 ml (¼ pint) double cream

salt and freshly ground black pepper

Preheat the oven to 160°C (325°F), gas mark 3.

Place the pumpkin, onion, garlic, thyme, olive oil, two-thirds of the almonds, chicken stock and salt and pepper in a large ovenproof dish and mix to make sure the pumpkin is well coated. Bake in the preheated oven and roast for about 40 minutes until the pumpkin is tender.

Tip the pumpkin and contents of the dish into a large saucepan, add the cream and, using a hand blender, purée until smooth (alternatively, blend in a food processor or blender). Check the seasoning.

Roughly chop the remaining almonds. Ladle the soup into serving bowls, top with the almonds and some extra thyme and serve immediately.

Nanna's bread

Nanna grew up in County Durham. She had two sisters and one brother. Her own mother died when she was 12 and so the girls had to take on the day-to-day running of the house. She talks so fondly of what were obviously very hard times, telling us how she used to make this bread before using the leftovers to make a 'bottom' or 'stottie cake'. Everything about Nanna is cosy and I still love sitting curled up next to her, hearing her stories of before and during the war and about the feasts they'd make with their rations. I must confess that before *Celebrity MasterChef* I'd never attempted to make bread. I was scared of it! But with my new-found confidence, I rang Nanna, got this recipe and Billie and I made a loaf and some rolls together one Sunday morning. I couldn't believe how simple it was and the house smelled amazing. There really is nothing like the smell and taste of freshly baked bread.

Makes 1 loaf

500 g (1 lb), strong white bread flour, plus extra for dusting

1 teaspoon sugar

1 teaspoon salt

1 x 7g sachet fast-action dried yeast

300 ml (½ pint) warm water

1 tablespoon oil

Mix the flour, sugar, salt and yeast together in a large mixing bowl. Slowly add the water, stirring the mixture until it comes away from the sides to form a dough.

Knead the dough on a floured surface until it is smooth and has elasticity – this should take about 10–15 minutes. Alternatively, if you have an electric mixer with a bread hook you can use this to knead the dough for the same amount of time. Cover the bowl with a damp cloth and leave it in a warm place (but not directly on top of a radiator!) for about 1 hour, or until it doubles in size.

Knead the dough for another 5–10 minutes and then transfer to an oiled bread tin. Cover and leave it for another 20–30 minutes. Meanwhile, preheat the oven to 220°C (425°F), gas mark 7.

Bake the loaf in the preheated oven for 25–30 minutes. When the bottom sounds hollow when tapped, it's ready. Leave to cool on a wire rack and eat it with real butter.

Sweet potato side dish

This recipe has been handed down to me by word of mouth from a Greek friend of mine – it's been in her family for years and I'm very honoured she has passed it on to me. It's delicious as a side dish, but also good as a main by adding some feta cheese to it about 10 minutes before the end of cooking.

Serves 4–6

1 tablespoon olive oil

2 red onions, sliced

about 4 sweet potatoes, sliced or cubed and par-boiled

1 x 185 g tin black olives, pitted

400 g baby tomatoes (or you can use 1 x 400 g tin chopped tomatoes)

1 x 190 g jar sun-dried tomato paste

a squirt of tomato purée

1 fresh thyme sprig, leaves only

½ cinnamon stick (remove before serving)

salt and freshly ground black pepper

extra virgin olive oil, for drizzling

Preheat the oven to 180°C (350°F), gas mark 4.

Heat the oil in a frying pan, add the onions and fry until softened and caramelised.

Put all the remaining ingredients in a mixing bowl and use your hands or a wooden spoon to make sure everything is evenly mixed and coated.

Transfer to an ovenproof dish, season and drizzle with extra virgin olive oil. Bake in the preheated oven for 45–60 minutes until soft and sticky.

Red cabbage

This is another recipe that my mum used to make in the 80s! My godmother, Nina, brings it over every Christmas. It is delicious with nearly everything, I think, but especially with Chicken Olives (see page 163) or shepherd's pie.

Serves 4–6

900 g (1 lb 13 oz) red cabbage, washed, trimmed and finely sliced

450 g (14½ oz) onions, chopped very small

450 g (14½ oz) cooking apples, peeled, cored and cut into small pieces

1 garlic clove, finely chopped

4 tablespoons chicken stock

3 tablespoons wine or cider vinegar

4 tablespoons redcurrant jelly

¼ teaspoon ground cinnamon

¼ teaspoon ground cloves

¼ teaspoon ground nutmeg

2 tablespoons brown sugar

15 ml (1 tablespoon) butter, softened

salt and freshly ground black pepper

Preheat the oven to 160°C (325°F), gas mark 3.

Put the cabbage into a large casserole dish with the onions, apples and garlic and pour over the stock and vinegar.

Add the redcurrant jelly, cinnamon, cloves, nutmeg and brown sugar. Mix thoroughly, cover with a lid and cook in the preheated oven for 1½ hours until the cabbage is very tender. Taste and season and add the butter before serving.

Note: Cooked red cabbage freezes very well; it will reheat beautifully, too, the same day or even a day later.

Stuffed courgettes

When I was growing up our garden was pretty overgrown and not particularly well tended, but a few times a year my dad would attempt to do something with it and grow rhubarb and courgettes and marrows. I don't know if he planted anything else but they are the only things I remember him growing. We had an abundance of these one year and luckily it was the 80s so it was very fashionable to stuff a marrow! I think courgettes are prettier and I like that these are individual portions.

Serves 4

4 large courgettes, weighing about 225 g (7½ oz) each

375 g (12 oz) minced lamb

1 small onion, chopped

2 garlic cloves, crushed

200 g (7 oz) passata

1 tablespoon tomato purée

1 teaspoon freshly chopped rosemary

1 teaspoon freshly chopped mint

a pinch of brown sugar

40 g (1½ oz) breadcrumbs (fresh or dried)

40 g (1½ oz) Parmesan cheese, grated

salt and freshly ground black pepper

finely chopped parsley, rosemary and mint, to finish

Preheat the oven to 190°C (375°F), gas mark 5.

Cut each courgette in half lengthways, scoop out the pulp into a bowl, leaving the outside shell about 1 cm (½ inch) thick.

Put the courgette shells in a roasting tin, cover with foil and bake in the preheated oven for about 12 minutes. They need to be tender but not too soft.

Put a frying pan over a medium heat and fry the minced lamb until browned. Add the onion and garlic and cook until softened, then add the courgette pulp, passata, tomato purée, rosemary, mint, sugar, salt and pepper. Stir together, bring to the boil and simmer gently for 10 minutes.

Mix the breadcrumbs and the Parmesan together in a small bowl. Spoon the stuffing mixture into the baked courgette shells and sprinkle with the Parmesan breadcrumbs. Return to the oven to bake for 20 minutes until golden and crispy on top. Finish with chopped parsley, rosemary and mint and serve.

This is one of the reasons I wanted to write a book like this! We all have family and friends that we get great recipes from and want to share.

Nanna Lily & Nanny Sue's green tomato pickle

My best friend Nicola always says she isn't a great cook, and in our twenties she was always the last one standing and came late to domesticity, but when she did, she did it wholeheartedly! She met her lovely man, Paul, and they have a beautiful family. Paul is ace at cooking – the first time I tried this pickle/chutney I made him write the recipe down straight away and promptly went home and made a batch. It's been in his family for generations and now has very kindly been passed on to me... and to you!

Makes 2 kg (4 lb)

750 g (1½ lb) green tomatoes

500 g (1 lb) cooking apples, peeled, cored and quartered

750 g (1½ lb) onions

900 ml (1½ pints) malt vinegar

750 g (1½ lb) soft brown sugar

25 g (1 oz) fresh ginger, peeled and grated

½ teaspoon turmeric

1 tablespoon salt

3 tablespoons cornflour

freshly ground black pepper

Put the tomatoes, apples and onions in a food processor or blender and pulse until finely chopped (alternatively, do this by hand and make sure everything is chopped into very small pieces).

Place the chopped vegetables in a large saucepan, then add 600 ml (1 pint) of the vinegar and the brown sugar and boil for 5 minutes.

Meanwhile, mix the ginger, turmeric, salt, some black pepper and cornflour with the remaining vinegar in a small bowl. Add this to the pan and boil again for 2 minutes.

Pour the chutney into clean, sterilised jars and seal. It will keep for up to 1 year stored in a cool, dark place.

Betty's damson jam

My dad's mother, Betty, was the queen of jam and pickles. She was my 'fun' grandma. She'd let us have a sip of her Cinzano at elevenses and tell us stories of her dancing days. Her larder was packed full of jam and marmalade, and what always amazed me was how immaculate everything was, even during the messy business of making jam! Her jams were always beautiful and just the right side of sweet.

Makes ten 500 g (1 lb) jars

3 kg (6 lb) damsons, stoned and halved (you can use Victoria plums instead, but I like to use damsons)

juice of 4 lemons

2.5 kg (5 lb) preserving sugar

Nanna's Bread (see page 142), to serve

Mix all of the ingredients together in a bowl or large saucepan and set aside at room temperature for 2 hours.

Transfer the ingredients to a large preserving pan, heat over a medium heat and bring to the boil. Keep boiling for about 15–20 minutes.

Test whether it is ready by dropping a small amount of the jam onto a cold plate. Push the jam with your finger – it should leave a film and 'wrinkle' on the plate. If it's not quite ready, carry on cooking for a few more minutes before testing again.

Take the pan off the heat and leave to cool for 10 minutes before transferring to sterilised jars and sealing. It will keep for up to 1 year stored in a cool, dark place.

Serve it with a fresh batch of Nanna's Bread.

Tomato ketchup

Why I feel I have to make tomato ketchup even though it comes in bottles of all sizes, I have no idea but, I love to cook and I want food that is cooked by me rather than bought. Christian O'Connell, my favourite DJ in the world, has been my guinea pig with this recipe. I have to listen to him every morning so I made him eat my ketchup and he said he liked it... oh and he loved my Bloody Mary, too, but who wouldn't at 7.30 in the morning?!

Makes about 500 ml (17 fl oz)

150 ml (¼ pint) red wine vinegar

1 blade of mace

½ teaspoon all-spice

2 cloves

4 x 400 g tins chopped tomatoes

2 onions, chopped

2 garlic cloves, chopped

100 ml (3½ fl oz) water

50 g (2 oz) muscovado sugar

Put the vinegar in a saucepan with the spices and cloves and heat for about 10 minutes over a low heat to infuse. Strain.

Put the tomatoes, onions, garlic, water, sugar and the strained infused vinegar into another saucepan and cook for about 40 minutes or so at a rolling boil until the mixture has reduced.

Pour into a food processor or blender (or blend with a hand blender) and blend until you have a smooth purée. If it is too thin after blending, put the liquid back in the saucepan over the heat and reduce until it reaches a thick sauce-like consistency.

Pour into warm, dry sterilised bottles and seal. The ketchup will keep in the fridge for 6 weeks once opened.

Fish & chips *with tartare sauce*

These are sort of 'healthy' fish and chips, because I love fish and chips, but not the guilt that goes with the grease and calories of them. I have used halibut because I prefer it to cod or haddock – it has a more delicate flavour and is a little bit different – but feel free to use whatever white fish you like. You will still need vinegar and lots of mayonnaise or tartare sauce and loads of salt... who said fish and chips were healthy?

Serves 4

4 baking potatoes

2–3 tablespoons olive oil, plus extra for greasing

1 tablespoon freshly chopped dill

100 g (3½ oz) breadcrumbs (fresh or dried)

grated rind of ½ lemon

flour, for dusting

1 egg, beaten

4 x responsibly sourced halibut fillets, weighing about 175 g (6 oz) each, skinned

salt and freshly ground black pepper

For the tartare sauce

100 g (3½ oz) Greek yogurt

25 g (1 oz) gherkins, chopped

½ garlic clove, crushed

grated rind of 1 lemon

juice of ½ lemon

10 g (⅓ oz) capers, chopped

a small bunch of fresh flat-leaf parsley, finely chopped

Preheat the oven to 190°C (375°F), gas mark 5 and line or grease two baking trays.

First, make the tartare sauce. Mix all of the ingredients in a bowl, adding salt and pepper to taste (you may not need much salt as the capers are salty). Set aside until needed.

Chop the potatoes into 'chunky chip'-sized pieces, leaving the skin on. Place in a large saucepan, cover with water and bring to the boil. Turn the heat down slightly and simmer for 2–3 minutes. Drain and place on one of the baking trays. Coat with the olive oil and season with salt and pepper. Bake in the preheated oven for 25–30 minutes, turning occasionally.

Meanwhile, prepare the fish. Mix the dill with the breadcrumbs and lemon rind in a shallow bowl. Put the flour and beaten egg in 2 separate shallow bowls. Dust each fillet of fish in the flour, then dip in the beaten egg and then the breadcrumb mix and place on the prepared baking tray. Bake in the preheated oven for 12–15 minutes, depending on thickness of the fillets.

Serve the fish with the chunky chips and tartare sauce.

Pan-fried sea bass & spicy rice

I think this book at times could be called 'The 80s on a Plate' it's so retro! Spicy rice was a real staple in our house served hot and then eaten cold as a salad the next day with a couple of crunchy peppers and some cucumber stirred through. What always makes me laugh is that we used to eat it cold the next day and Mummy would just put lots of spring onions and peppers in and pass it off as a new dinner! A funny memory!

Serves 4

4 x sea bass fillets, weighing about 125 g (4 oz) each, skin on and pin-boned

a good pinch of cayenne pepper

2 tablespoons oil

1 tablespoon butter

salt and freshly ground black pepper

For the rice

1 tablespoon sunflower oil

2 garlic cloves, finely chopped

2 tablespoons cumin seeds

a pinch of chilli flakes

250 g (8 oz) basmati rice, rinsed

450 ml (¾ pint) vegetable stock with a pinch of saffron added to it

1 x 400 g tin chickpeas, drained and rinsed

100 g (3½ oz) spinach, roughly chopped

30 g (1 oz) toasted coconut, plus extra to finish

1 tablespoon freshly chopped coriander, plus extra to finish

To make the rice, heat the oil in a large non-stick saucepan that has a lid and add the garlic, cumin seeds and chilli flakes and cook for about 30 seconds. Add the rice to the pan along with the stock and chickpeas and stir. Season and bring to the boil. Reduce to a medium heat, cover and cook for 15 minutes, until all the liquid has been absorbed and the rice is cooked.

Meanwhile, season the skin of the sea bass fillets with salt, pepper and cayenne. Heat a frying pan and add the oil. Fry the fish fillets, skin side down, in the hot pan for about 2–3 minutes. Turn the fish over, add the butter and cook for a further 2 minutes until cooked through.

Add the spinach to the rice and cook for a further minute. Sprinkle the rice with the toasted coconut and fresh coriander.

Cut the sea bass fillets in half and serve on a bed of spicy rice and finish with some more coconut and coriander if liked.

Chicken & mushroom pot pies

These pies are quick and easy to make, freeze very well and are delicious and warming when the wind is blowing outside!

Serves 4

3 x skinless chicken breasts, weighing about 200 g (7 oz) each, cut into strips

1 teaspoon plain flour, plus extra for dusting

25 g (1 oz) butter

1 tablespoon olive oil

2 shallots, chopped

300 g (10 oz) button mushrooms, cut into quarters

3 garlic cloves, chopped

½ teaspoon fennel seeds, crushed

125 ml (4 fl oz) chicken stock

100 ml (3½ fl oz) double cream

½ tablespoon freshly chopped tarragon

250 g (8 oz) chilled ready-made puff pastry

1 egg yolk

salt and freshly ground black pepper

Preheat the oven to 190°C (375°F), gas mark 5.

Put the chicken strips in a large plastic freezer bag, add the flour and some salt and pepper. Shake the bag so that the chicken is coated in the seasoned flour.

Melt half the butter with the olive oil in a frying pan and lightly brown the chicken. Remove with a slotted spoon and set aside.

Add the shallots, mushrooms, garlic and fennel seeds to the pan and fry until browned.

Add the stock and cream and boil to reduce until it has thickened enough to coat the back of a spoon. Add the tarragon, return the chicken to the pan and stir together.

Divide the chicken mix between 4 large ramekin dishes or 4 individual pans. Roll the pastry out on a lightly floured worksurface to about 1 cm (½ inch) thick. Cut out 4 rounds with a 12 cm (5 inch) round cutter and 4 rounds with a 2 cm (¾ inch) star cutter.

Brush the rim of the ramekin dishes or pans with egg yolk; place the larger pastry circle on top and the little pastry star in the middle. Brush the top with the remaining egg yolk and bake in the preheated oven for 20 minutes until puffed or golden.

Chicken tarragon

My absolute favourite dinner in the whole land was my mum's Chicken Tarragon. If ever my mum asked us what we wanted for dinner, a resounding 'Chicken tarragon!' was always our reply. She would serve it either with mash or pommes Anna (a French dish of sliced potatoes) and our plates would be licked clean. I would sit and just dip bread in the sauce, I loved it so much. What stays in my heart is that Mummy made this for us whenever she sensed we'd had a bad day or in celebration of passing exams or doing the school play. To me it's love on a plate.

Serves 4

50 g (2 oz) butter

4 x boneless chicken breasts, weighing about 200 g (7 oz) each, skin on

4 shallots, finely chopped

250 ml (8 fl oz) white wine

1 tablespoon tarragon vinegar

200 ml (7 fl oz) double cream

1 tablespoon freshly chopped tarragon

salt and freshly ground black pepper

Melt the butter in a large frying pan over a medium heat. Season the skin of the chicken breasts and place them, skin side down, in the butter and cook for about 10 minutes until the skin is crispy. Turn the chicken over, lower the heat a little and then cook for a further 10 minutes or until the chicken is cooked through. Use a slotted spoon to transfer the chicken to a plate to rest.

Fry the shallots in the pan for 1–2 minutes and then add the wine and tarragon vinegar and boil to reduce by half. Add the cream and let it bubble away until thickened. Stir through the tarragon and season.

Place the chicken breasts in a serving dish and pour over the tarragon sauce before serving with your choice of potatoes.

Chicken olives *with parmentier potatoes*

This is one of those recipes that hold secrets that only sisters know about. We have certain things that we call 'Lifeboat Food': when I am drowning Victoria comes to my rescue and this chicken is, and has been, the buoy that has kept us both from drowning... For Toria.

Serves 4–6

For the chicken olives

1 x large boneless and skinless chicken breast fillet, weighing about 200 g (7 oz)

1 large garlic clove

2.5 cm (1 inch) piece of fresh ginger, peeled

1 tablespoon flat-leaf parsley

1 teaspoon fennel seeds

1 teaspoon coriander seeds, toasted

65 g (2½ oz) chorizo, chopped

8 x boneless chicken thigh fillets, skin on

olive oil, for rubbing

salt and freshly ground black pepper

For the parmentier potatoes

25 g (1 oz) butter

400 g (13 oz) potatoes, cut into 1 cm (½ inch) cubes

2 garlic cloves, chopped

2 fresh rosemary sprigs, leaves taken off stalks and chopped

1 tablespoon freshly chopped flat-leaf parsley

2 tablespoons olive oil

Preheat the oven to 180°C (350°F), gas mark 4.

To make the chicken olives, place the chicken breast in a food processor or blender and whizz until minced. Transfer to a bowl.

Next, chop the garlic, ginger, parsley and fennel and coriander seeds in the food processor or blender (or chop very finely by hand). Add this mix, along with the chorizo, salt and pepper to the minced chicken and combine well.

Place the chicken thighs, skin side down, on a board and spoon about 2 teaspoons of the chicken mix in the middle of each thigh. Roll up and secure each one with a cocktail stick.

Place the stuffed thighs onto a baking tray, rub with olive oil, season with salt and pepper and bake in the preheated oven for 40 minutes, until the skin is crispy and the chicken is cooked through.

While the chicken is cooking, make the potatoes. Heat the butter in a large frying pan, add the potatoes and cook for 5 minutes over a medium heat. Add the chopped garlic and cook for a further 5 minutes until the potatoes have softened. Mix in the rosemary and the parsley and transfer to a baking tray. Pour over the oil to coat the potatoes, season and bake in the preheated oven for about 25–30 minutes until crispy and tender.

Serve the parmentier potatoes with the 1–2 baked chicken olives per serving.

Victoria's lasagne

I think Victoria and I started cooking properly when my mum died. Before, we had watched, and thankfully absorbed, a lot of my mum's recipes and methods, but suddenly (well it seemed sudden) we were thrown into adulthood. I was 16 and thought I knew everything and Victoria was 14, and thought she did, too! We quickly took it upon ourselves to cook as much as possible to help my dad out. Whenever I've travelled or been away from home for any length of time I ask Victoria to cook this and I'm instantly 'home again'.

Serves 6

250 g (8 oz) dried lasagne sheets

25 g (1 oz) Parmesan, finely grated

For the meat sauce

2 tablespoons olive oil

1 large onion, finely chopped

2 garlic cloves, finely sliced

500 g (1 lb) lean minced steak

3 tablespoons tomato purée

1 x 400 g tin chopped tomatoes

1 beef stock cube, dissolved in about 2 tablespoons boiling water

1 teaspoon Marmite

a dash of Worcestershire sauce

salt and freshly ground black pepper

For the white sauce

500 ml (17 fl oz) milk

1 onion, peeled

2 cloves, studded into the onion

2 fresh bay leaves

6 peppercorns

50 g (2 oz) unsalted butter

50 g (2 oz) plain flour

1 tablespoon grated Cheddar cheese (optional)

a dash of Worcestershire sauce

To make the meat sauce, heat the oil in a large frying pan or saucepan and fry the onion until browned. Add the garlic and cook for a couple more minutes.

Add the mince and cook until browned, breaking up the lumps with a spoon as you stir. Drain off any fat, but try to retain the meat juices if possible.

Add the tomato purée and stir in thoroughly, then add the tinned tomatoes, beef stock paste, Marmite, a good glug of Worcestershire sauce and season with salt and pepper. Bring this to the boil, reduce the heat and then simmer for about 30 minutes. (I have been known to cook this for hours over a very low heat, but 30 minutes is the minimum to let all the flavours infuse.)

Meanwhile, make the white sauce. Put the milk, onion (studded with cloves), bay leaves and peppercorns into a saucepan over a moderate heat and bring up to a simmer. Do not let it boil. Turn off the heat and leave to infuse for 10 minutes, then strain and discard the bits.

In a separate saucepan, melt the butter, then add the flour gradually, whisking it in until you have a smooth roux. Cook for about 4–5 minutes.

Add a quarter of the hot strained milk and bring to the boil, whisking to get rip of the lumps. Add half of the milk left in the pan and whisk again so there are no lumps and then finally add the remaining milk. Bring to the boil and cook for 5 minutes making sure there are no lumps and you cannot taste the flour.

Stir in the Cheddar cheese, if using and the Worcestershire sauce and season to taste. Take off the heat.

Preheat the oven to 190°C (375°F), gas mark 5.

In a medium-sized ovenproof dish add a layer of the cooked meat sauce, then cover with a single layer of lasagne sheets, then pour over the white sauce. Repeat this process, finishing with a layer of white sauce. You should get about 3 layers of lasagne.

Sprinkle over the Parmesan cheese and bake in the preheated oven for 30 minutes until it is golden and crispy on top. Test to see if the lasagne is cooked by piercing with a sharp knife. If the knife goes in with little resistance, the lasagne is soft and cooked. Leave the lasagne to rest, covered, for 10 minutes before serving.

Note: The meat sauce can be made well in advance, in fact, it always seems to taste better the following day, then you can 'build' your lasagne just before you want to eat it.

One of the first dishes I remember Toria making after our mum died was this lasagne. It quickly became a weekly favourite, and we've cooked it ever since.

Pork with cider

This recipe is actually a collaboration of my mother-in-law Margaret's recipe and my oldest friend Emma's mother-in-law's recipe – plus a little bit of what I think works. I love how recipes get passed down and around and played with to suit people's tastes and what they have to hand in their storecupboard. That to me is what cooking, and this book, is all about. So, thank you to the mother-in-laws!

Serves 4–6

About 600 g (1 lb 2 oz) pork fillet, cut into 5 cm (2 inch) thick pieces

1 tablespoon olive oil

8 banana shallots, peeled and cut into quarters

3 garlic cloves, chopped

1 large cooking apple, peeled, quartered and sliced

150 ml (¼ pint) dry cider

300 ml (½ pint) chicken stock

2 tablespoons wholegrain mustard

1 teaspoon honey

100 ml (3½ fl oz) double cream

2 tablespoons freshly chopped flat-leaf parsley

salt and freshly ground black pepper

Preheat the oven to 160°C (325°F), gas mark 3.

Season the pork. Heat a large casserole dish with the oil and fry the pork until browned all over.

Add the shallots, garlic and apple and brown. Add the cider, stock, mustard and honey, mix together and check the seasoning. Cover and put in the preheated oven for about 20 minutes until the pork is tender and cooked through.

Use a slotted spoon to remove the pork from the casserole, set aside, cover and keep warm.

Add the cream to the sauce, return to the hob and boil and reduce until the sauce is thickened, about 5 minutes.

Return the pork to the casserole and stir through the parsley.

Macaroni cheese

This is our perfect autumn Saturday lunch. Billie asks for it constantly! I first fell in love with macaroni cheese when I was living in America. When I was feeling homesick I would make it, find English programmes on BBC America and sit and eat a large bowlful while pretending I was at home in England.

Serves 4–6

300 g (10 oz) macaroni

75 g (3 oz) pancetta, cubed

2 leeks, trimmed and thinly sliced

50 g (2 oz) butter

50 g (2 oz) plain flour

600 ml (1 pint) milk

1 teaspoon mustard powder

a dash of Worcestershire sauce

225 g (7½ oz) Cheddar cheese, grated

75 g (3 oz) Parmesan cheese, grated

65 g (2½ oz) breadcrumbs (fresh or dried)

salt and freshly ground black pepper

Preheat the oven to 190°C (375°F), gas mark 5.

Bring a large saucepan of salted water to the boil and cook the macaroni for 10 minutes, then drain.

In a small frying pan, brown the pancetta over a medium heat, add the leeks and fry until softened but not browned. Set aside.

Melt the butter in a saucepan and add the flour, beating with a wooden spoon to form a roux. Cook this for 1–2 minutes, stirring all the time.

Add the milk little by little, stirring all the time until the sauce is thickened, then add the mustard powder, Worcestershire sauce and salt and pepper. Take the pan off the heat and stir in the grated Cheddar and Parmesan cheese until combined.

Mix the leeks and pancetta into the macaroni and then spoon into a large ovenproof dish. Pour over the cheese sauce and sprinkle over the breadcrumbs. Bake in the preheated oven for 25 minutes, until bubbling and crispy on top.

Slow-cooked chilli con carne

Our house was always bustling and my mum didn't need much of an excuse for a get-together. In the 1980s, Halloween was not as widely celebrated as it is today, but my mum was obsessed with America, and what was good enough for the US was good enough for us! As a result we were the first kids on our street to go trick or treating! This was a great favourite at Halloween parties, served with rice or a crispy-skinned jacket potato.

Serves 4–6

2 tablespoons olive oil

1 kg (2 lb) beef stewing steak, cut into pieces

200 g (7 oz) chorizo, sliced

2 large onions, chopped

4 garlic cloves, finely sliced

2 teaspoons ground cumin

2 teaspoons all-spice

1 bay leaf

1 teaspoon cayenne pepper

1 dried red chilli, chopped

2 x 400 g tins chopped tomatoes

1 tablespoon tomato purée

2 tablespoons tomato ketchup

3 tablespoons balsamic vinegar

1 tablespoon sugar (any kind)

200 ml (7 fl oz) red wine or beef stock

1 x 400 g tin kidney beans, drained and rinsed

2 tablespoons freshly chopped coriander (optional)

salt and freshly ground black pepper

Preheat the oven to 160°C (325°F), gas mark 3.

Heat the oil in a frying pan or a large casserole dish. Fry the meat on all sides until golden. Use a slotted spoon to remove the meat from the pan and set aside.

Put the chorizo into the pan and brown until it just starts to release its juices. Use a slotted spoon again to remove the chorizo and set aside, reserving the oil in the pan.

Fry the onion, garlic, spices, herbs and chilli in the chorizo oil until softened. Season and add the tomatoes, tomato purée, ketchup, balsamic vinegar and sugar. Stir until mixed.

Put the beef and chorizo back in the pan along with the wine or stock. Bring up to simmering point and cover with the lid. Transfer to the preheated oven and cook for 2 hours. Take out of the oven, add the kidney beans and return to the oven for a further hour. Stir through the coriander, if using, before serving.

Beef Wellington

This story seems fitting the year I am going to be 40. I remember my mum's 40th birthday so well, and can't quite believe I have reached that age. It was the autumn of 1984 and there was a great fuss made about my mother turning 40. We had 'Life begins at 40' banners and Victoria and I made her a birthday cake in the shape of a baby's bottle! She had a big lunch with her girlfriends and a dinner party that my godmother, Ann, hosted. Starters were smoked salmon parcels, followed by individual Beef Wellingtons. Mummy said that Ann was the queen of these. They may seem fiddly, because there are lots of different bits to the recipe, but when you break it down all the steps are pretty straightforward, and the recipe is well worth the effort.

Serves 6

200 g (7 oz) chicken liver pâté

700 g (1 lb 6 oz) beef fillet

1 x 400 g large sheet of puff pastry

1 egg, beaten

salt and freshly ground black pepper

For the mushroom duxelle mix

200 g (7 oz) mixed mushrooms

50 g (2 oz) butter

1 onion, diced

3 garlic cloves, chopped

3 tablespoons freshly chopped sage

3 tablespoons freshly chopped thyme

For the pancakes

200 g (7 oz) plain flour

3 eggs

300 ml (½ pint) milk

25 g (1 oz) butter, for frying

Preheat the oven to 190°C (375°F), gas mark 5. Make the mushroom duxelle mix. Put the mixed mushrooms in a food processor or blender and pulse to a rough dice. Heat the butter in a frying pan and fry the onion and garlic until softened but not coloured. Add the chopped mushrooms and cook, again without colouring, for 5 minutes. Season, then add the thyme and sage. Leave to cool.

Next, make the pancakes. Mix the ingredients in a jug. Heat the butter in a small frying pan and pour two-thirds of it into a small bowl to keep aside for brushing the pan in between pancakes. Pour a small amount of the batter into the frying pan and swirl it around to cover the base of the pan. Cook for 1–2 minutes and then flip and cook for another minute. Remove the pancake from the pan to a plate and continue to cook 5 more pancakes. Layer the pancakes with greaseproof paper in between and leave to cool.

Season and seal the beef fillet and set aside. Mix the cooled mushroom duxelle with the pâté in a mixing bowl. Brush the large sheet of pastry with the egg wash. Layer the pancakes over the top of the pastry so that it is covered and then use a palate knife to spread the mushroom mixture on top. Place the beef fillet on top of the mushroom mixture and roll up the pastry, making sure that the beef is completely surrounded by the mushroom mix and the pancakes and well sealed. Leave to chill.

Place the Wellington on a baking tray and brush the top with beaten egg. Bake in the oven for 30 minutes, or to your liking.

Beef bourguignon

Everyone has their own version of this dish. We had a slow cooker at home and my mum used it a lot (I do, too). She would tip everything into it before going to work in the mornings, and by the time we came back from school the smell of the Beef Bourguignon would have filled the house. It freezes well and my godmother, Nina, used to bring it over to our house in the early days of adopting Billie, to give me a break from cooking.

Serves 4–6

500 g (1 lb) diced beef or stewing steak

flour, for dusting

olive oil, for frying

200 g (7 oz) pancetta or streaky bacon lardons

300 g (10 oz) shallots, peeled and halved at the root

3 garlic cloves

2 tablespoons tomato purée

125 g (4 oz) chestnut or button mushrooms

500 ml (17 fl oz) full-bodied Burgundy red wine

250 ml (8 fl oz) beef stock

1 bouquet garni (dried or freshly made with parsley, thyme, rosemary and bay)

salt and freshly ground black pepper

creamy mustard mash, to serve (optional)

Preheat the oven to 160°C (325°F), gas mark 3.

Place the beef in a large plastic freezer bag and add some flour and salt and pepper. Shake until the beef is coated in the seasoned flour.

Heat a good glug of oil in a large casserole dish and brown the meat in batches (about 2 minutes on each side). Use a slotted spoon to remove the meat from the casserole and set aside.

In the same casserole, add the lardons, shallots and garlic and fry until brown. Add the tomato purée and mushrooms and mix through. Return the beef to the casserole and add the wine, stock and bouquet garni. Bring to the boil (make sure you scrape the bottom of the casserole to get all the lovely juices and crispy bits).

Cover the casserole with a lid and cook in the preheated oven for a good 3 hours. Serve with a creamy mustard mash, if liked.

Note: This can also be cooked in a slow cooker once the meat has been browned.

Boeuf en daube

This is a really hearty dish, perfect for cold evenings.

Serves 4

2 tablespoons olive oil

25 g (1 oz) unsalted butter

1 kg (2 lb) beef brisket, cut into 6 cm (2½ inch) pieces

1 large onion, chopped

2 garlic cloves, crushed

1 x 400 g tin chopped tomatoes

150 ml (¼ pint) red wine

1 tablespoon freshly chopped thyme

grated rind 1 orange

125 g (4 oz) green olives, pitted

salt and freshly ground black pepper

Preheat the oven to 160°C (325°F), gas mark 3.

In a large casserole dish, heat the oil, then add the butter. Once the butter is foaming, add the beef in batches and cook for a few minutes until browned, Remove the beef with a slotted spoon and set aside, then add the onion and garlic and cook until softened, about 5 minutes.

Add the tomatoes, wine, thyme, orange rind and salt and pepper. Bring to the boil, then cover and put in the preheated oven for 2–2½ hours.

Use a slotted spoon to remove the beef from the casserole and set aside to rest. Put the casserole over a high heat, add the olives and boil and reduce the sauce for 5–10 minutes until the sauce has thickened. Check and adjust the seasoning if necessary.

Return the beef to the casserole, stir through and serve.

Salted crème caramel

Nearly every year we went on a package holiday to Spain. All very last minute, my mum would suddenly decide we could afford a holiday and that she needed to see the sun, so we would race down to the travel agents where they would be doing some last-minute deal and we would be flying to Alicante that evening or the next morning. She was very impulsive! These holidays were always on a shoestring, but we loved them. We would eat in every other night and so there were a lot of trips to the Spanish supermarkets – I loved the smell of them and all the different foods on offer. We always used to buy crème caramels because they were my dad's and my favourite dessert. The custard was so smooth, but there never seemed to be enough caramel. Years on, I'm still making these for my daddy and myself, though I now have an addiction to salted caramel, so decided to try it on top of the custard. I think it's truly delicious, but you can always leave out the salt if you want.

Makes 6

For the salted caramel

175 g (6 oz) caster sugar

2 tablespoons water

2 pinches of sea salt

For the crème

300 ml (½ pint) whole milk

275 ml (9 fl oz) single cream

1 vanilla pod, split lengthways

2 whole eggs

3 egg yolks

100 g (3½ oz) caster sugar

Preheat the oven to 150°C (300°F), gas mark 2. To make the caramel, boil the sugar, water and salt together in a small saucepan without stirring for 5–6 minutes, until the syrup thickens and caramelises and turns a light golden brown. Watch it – you don't want it to turn too dark otherwise it will just be rock hard! Pour immediately into 6 dariole moulds or ramekins.

For the crème, put the milk and cream in a saucepan and scrape the seeds from the split vanilla pod into it. Drop in the empty pod, too, and warm gently to a simmer, then take off the heat. Whisk the eggs and sugar in a bowl. Pass the milk mixture through a sieve into the whisked eggs and sugar and mix together quickly. Pour the mixture into the caramel-filled moulds.

Place the moulds in a roasting tin and pour hot water around the moulds until it reaches halfway up the sides. Bake in the oven for about 40 minutes. Remove, set aside and cool for 1 hour before putting them in the fridge to set for a further 4 hours or overnight. To serve, turn the moulds out onto serving bowls and let the salted caramel drip down over the deliciously set crème.

Note: To stop the caramel from hardening, place the saucepan in a tray of cold water. To clean saucepans and remove any remaining hardened caramel, place the pan back on the heat with a little washing up liquid and water and heat gently for about 10 minutes.

Vanilla rice pudding
with blackberry compote

Warm, creamy, sweet, vanilla, fruity loveliness... no more needs to be said!

Makes 6

For the rice pudding

600 ml (1 pint) whole milk

300 ml (½ pint) double cream

50 g (2 oz) vanilla sugar or caster sugar, plus a little extra for sprinkling

1 vanilla pod, split lengthways

125 g (4 oz) pudding rice

For the compote

150 g (5 oz) blackberries

50 g (2 oz) caster sugar

2 tablespoons crème de cassis

Preheat the oven to 160°C (325°F), gas mark 3.

Put the milk, cream and sugar in a large saucepan. Scrape the seeds from the split vanilla pod into the pan and drop in the empty pod, too. Bring to a simmer.

Add the rice and then cook over a low heat, stirring occasionally so the rice doesn't stick, for about 45–60 minutes, or until the rice has thickened.

Meanwhile, make the compote. Put all of the compote ingredients in a small saucepan and let it bubble over a medium heat until the blackberries have softened and the sugar and cassis have combined and thickened, about 5–10 minutes. Pass the mixture through a sieve.

Put a spoonful of the blackberry compote into the bottom of 6 small bowls or ramekin dishes, top with the rice pudding and sprinkle with a little extra sugar. Cook in the preheated oven for about 15–20 minutes. Serve immediately.

When my parents got married, my grandma gave my mum a list of my dad's favourite dinners, with instructions on how to cook them – my sister and I have always thought it was hilarious!

Treacle tart & vanilla ice cream

This is my dad's favourite pudding. My grandma used to say my dad was 'the top brick off the chimney', she spoilt him rotten and she wanted my mum to do the same. You would easily be forgiven for thinking that my dad would have been a right piece of work with that sort of upbringing, but he isn't. He is the kindest, most unassuming man you could ever meet. He has supported me through thick and thin, keeping his opinions of some of my big life decisions to himself, unless asked for his advice. I wish I had inherited some of his level-headedness and calm! Anyway, this treacle tart was on 'the list' – it's chewy and sweet and salty, and vanilla ice cream really complements it.

Serves 6

250 g (8 oz) golden syrup

juice of ½ lemon

75 g (3 oz) dried white breadcrumbs

25 g (1 oz) cornflakes

For the pastry

300 g (10 oz) plain flour, plus extra for dusting

150 g (5 oz) cold butter, cubed

1 tablespoon cold water

a pinch of salt

For the ice cream

500 ml (17 fl oz) whole milk

1 vanilla pod, split lengthways

8 egg yolks

225 g (7½ oz) caster sugar

300 ml (½ pint) double cream

First, make the ice cream. Put the milk in a saucepan and scrape in the seeds from the split vanilla pod and drop in the empty pod too. Gently bring to the boil. Whisk the egg yolks and sugar together in a mixing bowl. Add the boiled milk to the eggs, whisking thoroughly until mixed. Leave to cool. Just before churning in an ice-cream maker, strain and add the cream. Alternatively, add the cream and mix thoroughly, then pour into an airtight container. Freeze for 1 hour, then remove from the freezer and break up any ice crystals with a fork. Return to the freezer and repeat this process over the next 4 hours until you have a smooth ice cream.

Meanwhile, make the pastry. Put the flour, butter and salt in a food processor and whizz for about 10 seconds until the mixture resembles fine breadcrumbs. Use the pulse button to avoid over-working the mixture. Add the water and whizz again for 2–3 seconds until the ingredients begin to stick. Collect the mixture together with lightly floured hands and knead lightly on a floured surface for 20–30 seconds. Shape the dough into a flat disc. Wrap in cling film and chill for 30 minutes before using.

Roll the pastry out on a lightly floured surface to about 5 mm (¼ inch) thick. Use it to line an 18 cm (7 inch) loose-bottomed fluted flan tin. Preheat the oven to 180°C (350°F), gas mark 4.

For the filling, combine the syrup, lemon juice and breadcrumbs in a mixing bowl and then spoon this into the pastry case. Crush the cornflakes lightly with your hands and sprinkle them over the top of the tart. Bake in the preheated oven for 20 minutes until golden brown. Serve with the vanilla ice cream.

Sunshine shorties

These biscuits are properly melt-in-the-mouth delicious. I have been making them since I was about seven years old and passed my Brownie Hostess Badge with them!

Makes about 15

125 g (4 oz) butter, plus extra for greasing

125 g (4 oz) caster sugar

1 teaspoon golden syrup

1 teaspoon bicarbonate of soda

1 teaspoon boiling water

125 g (4 oz) porridge oats

125 g (4 oz) self-raising flour

Preheat the oven to 160°C (325°F), gas mark 3 and grease a baking tray.

Put the butter, sugar, syrup, bicarbonate of soda and water into a large saucepan and melt. Take off the heat, add the oats and flour and stir to combine.

Place teaspoon-sized balls on the prepared baking tray, leaving space between them to spread out.

Bake in the preheated oven for 10–15 minutes until browned. Cool on a wire rack.

They are incredibly simple
and a Faulkner family favourite!

My mum would always make these teas into an occasion, using her best china and making sandwiches, scones, cakes and these hazelnut meringues.

Hazelnut meringues

Sundays, especially in autumn and winter, could seem quite gloomy and heavy with that 'school tomorrow' feeling. I know I suffer from winter blues and my mum did too. Her way of combatting them and chasing them away was to keep the house full and keep cooking. My Great-auntie Elsie spent practically every weekend at ours because she was on her own, and my Nanna and Lely would come over for tea. Autumn to me is filled with these Sunday memories, my dad building bonfires and raking away the leaves, us off on the common with our bikes, cycling home smelling of bonfires, and scrabbling to get our homework done and bath and hairwash before *Bread* started on the television.

Makes 6–8 sandwiched meringues

butter, for greasing

4 egg whites

250 g (8 oz) caster sugar

1 teaspoon white wine vinegar

100 g (3½ oz) ground hazelnuts, toasted

250 ml (8 fl oz) double cream, whisked until thick

Preheat the oven to 140°C (275°F), gas mark 1 and grease and line 1–2 baking trays.

Whisk the egg whites in a large, clean bowl, either by hand or with a hand-held electric mixer, until soft peaks form. Gradually whisk in the sugar until the egg whites turn glossy and form stiff peaks. Add the vinegar and fold in.

Using a large metal spoon, gently fold in 75 g (3 oz) of the hazelnuts (reserving the rest to sprinkle on top). Spoon the mixture (about 12–16 dessertspoon-sized 'balls') onto the prepared baking tray(s).

Bake in the preheated oven for 1 hour until crisp and then cool on wire racks.

When the meringues are cool, sandwich them together with the cream and sprinkle the remaining hazelnuts on top.

Pistachio & rosewater biscotti

These got me through IVF! I'd make bucketloads and dip them into numerous cups of tea while keeping my legs and everything else crossed on the sofa!

Makes 20

110 g (3½ oz) plain flour

½ teaspoon baking powder

50 g (2 oz) cold butter, cubed, plus extra for greasing

75 g (3 oz) soft brown sugar

50 g (2 oz) pistachios, chopped

3 teaspoons rosewater

1 egg white

Preheat the oven to 160°C (325°F), gas mark 3 and grease a baking tray.

Sieve the flour and baking powder into a food processor and add the butter and sugar and pulse until the mixture resembles breadcrumbs.

Turn the mixture out into a large bowl, add the pistachios, then the rosewater and egg white and knead.

Shape the dough into a long sausage and put on the prepared baking tray. Bake in the preheated oven for 30 minutes.

Leave to cool for 15 minutes, slice on the angle and cut into about 20 slices. Return the slices back to the baking tray and cook in the oven for a further 10 minutes until golden and crispy.

Mummy's quick & easy chocolate cake

Whenever it was anyone's birthday, my mum would make this cake. It seemed to take her no time at all, and if it wasn't cut into all sorts of different shapes for whatever 'theme' we wanted, then it would be iced with shiny chocolate. It would always look pretty when she did this, and I often thought I would like that for my birthday cake, but for some reason I never told her that.

Serves 8–10

For the cake

175 g (6 oz) unsalted butter, softened, plus extra for greasing

175 g (6 oz) caster sugar

3 large eggs

175 g (6 oz) self-raising flour

1½ teaspoons baking powder

2 tablespoons drinking chocolate

1 tablespoon warm water

For the filling

125 g (4 oz) icing sugar

1½ oz unsalted butter, softened

1 tablespoon whole milk

For the icing

250 g (8 oz) dark chocolate, broken into pieces and melted

15 g (½ oz) unsalted butter, softened

To decorate (optional)

glacé cherries, halved

sliced almonds

Preheat the oven to 180°C (350°F), gas mark 4 and grease two 20 cm (8 inch) shallow cake tins.

Mix all of the cake ingredients together in a large mixing bowl until thoroughly amalgamated. Pour into the prepared cake tins and shake gently to level the surface.

Bake the cakes in the preheated oven for 20 minutes, or until the top springs back when pushed with your finger. Turn the cakes out onto a wire rack and leave to cool.

Meanwhile, make the filling and the icing. Mix all of the filling ingredients together in a mixing bowl. In a separate bowl, stir the melted chocolate and the butter together and beat well until thoroughly mixed.

When the cakes are cool, lay one of the shallow layers on a serving plate. Spread the filling mixture across the cake and top with the second layer. Spread the icing on the top half of the cake and use a palette knife to smooth it out and down the sides until it is all completely covered. Decorate with glacé cherries and almonds, if liked.

...it would be iced with shiny chocolate
and little flowers my mum had made out of toasted
almonds and cherries.

Winter

Betty's orange marmalade

Going to stay at my grandma, Betty's was always an adventure. Her house was in-between countryside and the sea. After a long car journey we were always greeted by the smell of baking and Betty telling us to go and have a run in the garden and get some fresh air. I remember waking up in the mornings to the sound of wood pigeons and the 'Teasmade'! Betty would always bring Victoria and me a cup of tea in bed and we'd sit up in our beds feeling very grown-up with the smell of bacon grilling downstairs. The smell of my house when I make marmalade transports me back in time to our wonderful weekends and holidays at Betty's.

Right – marmalade is a tricky business! The first time I attempted a batch I burnt it (although it made a great glaze for my gammon). I didn't realise you had to watch it, to care for it a bit more than when you're making jam.

Makes about ten 500 g (1 lb) jars

1.5 kg (3 lb) Seville oranges

1 lemon

3.6 litres (6 pints) water

3 kg (6 lb) preserving sugar

Halve the oranges and the lemon and squeeze the juice through a sieve into a big preserving pan (make sure it is a preserving pan – it needs a heavy base and it needs to be deep).

Once all the oranges and the lemon have been squeezed, put the pips and all the white pith you can scrape out and all contents of the sieve into a muslin bag and tie tightly. (To get all the pith, quarter the orange skins and scrape the pith off with a knife until you're pretty much just left with the orange peel.)

Put all the orange peel in a food processor or blender and chop to your desired thickness.

Transfer the chopped peel to the preserving pan along with the muslin bag and the water. Bring to the boil, squeezing the muslin bag occasionally. Cook for 1½–2 hours.

Remove the muslin bag, put it in a sieve over the pan and squeeze out as much juice as possible with a potato masher – it is important to squeeze out the bag as it contains all the pectin, which will make the marmalade set. Discard the bag.

Tip the preserving sugar into the pan and cook over a low heat, stirring until the sugar is dissolved. Do not be tempted to do this too fast – slowly, slowly!

Breakfast was always delicious, a soft-boiled egg, bacon and a piece of perfectly fried bread, followed by toast and Betty's homemade marmalade.

Once the sugar has dissolved, boil the mixture rapidly for about 20–30 minutes until you reach setting point. The mixture will bubble right up. Watch this step – you need to make sure it doesn't burn. I test the jam on a cold plate – put a spoonful of the marmalade on a plate, it should wrinkle when you push it with your finger. If it doesn't, then continue to cook for a further 5–10 minutes and then test again. I also use a jam thermometer to check that the jam has reached 105°C (220°F). It takes approximately 30 minutes. Take off the heat.

Leave the marmalade in the pan for 10 minutes, skim off the froth and pour into clean, sterilised jars and use discs and cellophane tops to seal. The marmalade will keep for up to 1 year stored in a cool, dark place.

I also didn't realise the importance of the squeezing of the muslin bag – all these things I wish Betty had been around to tell me.

Piccalilli

My grandma and granddad, Betty and Norman, lived in West Sussex and owned a beach hut on West Wittering beach. Rain or shine our Easter, summer, Christmas and half-term holidays were spent on that beach, splashing in the sea, making dens in the hedgerows, collecting pebbles and watching the world go by while eating corned beef and piccalilli sandwiches and jam tarts. It's funny because I especially liked the beach in winter, the wind whistling round our ears and the waves crashing. We would be sitting on our deckchairs on the beach hut veranda with blankets over our legs and flasks of hot tea. Whenever I need to clear my head I go to West Wittering and sit on the veranda at the beach hut that once belonged to my family.

Betty never put coriander seeds in her piccalilli but I love them and if I had my way they would be in practically everything I make. My family and friends love my Piccalilli and I find myself making huge vats of it around Christmas time to give out to them all.

Makes about 2 kg (4 lb)

1 litre (1¾ pints) malt vinegar

3 tablespoons coriander seeds

1 tablespoon fennel seeds

1 large cauliflower, cut into small florets

2 large onions, chopped finely

4½ tablespoons mustard powder

4½ tablespoons plain flour

1½ tablespoons turmeric

3 tablespoons ground ginger

200 ml (7 fl oz) cider vinegar

125 g (4 oz) French beans, chopped into 1 cm (½ inch) pieces

2 red peppers, deseeded and chopped into 1 cm (½ inch) pieces

1 cucumber, diced

3 garlic cloves, finely sliced

250 g (8 oz) caster sugar

Put the malt vinegar, coriander seeds and fennel seeds into a large preserving pan and bring to the boil. Add the cauliflower and onions, and cook until softened, but so that they still have a bit of 'bite' to them.

Mix the mustard powder, flour, turmeric, ginger and cider vinegar together in a bowl until you have a smooth paste.

Add the French beans, red peppers, cucumber, garlic and sugar to the pan and lightly simmer until the sugar is dissolved. Drain over a large pan or bowl and reserve the vinegar liquid.

Put the mustard paste into the large pan containing the vinegar liquid and bring to the boil. Reduce the temperature and simmer until thick enough to coat the back of a spoon. Transfer the vegetables back to the large pan and mix until combined.

Spoon the piccalilli into clean, sterilised jars and seal. It will keep for up to 1 year in a cool, dark place.

Goat's cheese & red onion tart
with thyme pastry

This was my winning starter for *Celebrity MasterChef*. I wanted to make it different and thought thyme would be lovely in the pastry. Sometimes it's just a case of taking the simple things and adding something to make it that extra bit special.

Serves 4

For the pastry

1 small thyme sprig

100 g (3½ oz) plain flour, plus extra for dusting

25 g (1 oz) cold butter, cubed

25 g (1 oz) cold lard, cubed

2–3 tablespoons water

For the red onion jam

25 g (1 oz) butter

25 g (1 oz) soft brown sugar

1 tablespoon balsamic vinegar

1–2 tablespoons of crème de cassis

2 red onions, finely sliced

salt and freshly ground black pepper

For the goat's cheese

175 g (6 oz) crumbly goat's cheese

1 egg yolk

1–2 tablespoons double cream

For the salad

a handful of rocket leaves

2 tablespoons olive oil

2 teaspoons lemon juice

To make the pastry, strip the thyme leaves into a food processor or blender and add the flour, butter and lard. Mix on the pulse setting until it resembles breadcrumbs. Gradually add enough cold water to form a soft dough. Wrap in cling film and chill for about 30 minutes.

To make the onion jam, melt the butter in a sauté pan and add the sugar, vinegar, cassis and some seasoning. Add the onions, bring to the boil and cook, uncovered, over a very low heat for 30 minutes. Preheat the oven to 200°C (400°F), gas mark 6 and place a sturdy baking tray in the oven.

Divide the pastry into quarters and roll out on a lightly floured surface to form circles large enough to line four 10 cm (4 inch) loose-bottomed tart tins. Line each pastry case with baking paper and baking beans. Place on the heated baking tray and cook for 10 minutes. Remove the beans and lining paper and return to the oven for 5 minutes. Leave to cool for a few minutes.

Trim away any rind on the goat's cheese and crumble the cheese into a bowl. Mix with the egg yolk and a splash of cream and season with salt and pepper.

Reserve about one-third of the red onion jam to use as garnish, then divide the rest between the tartlets and spoon the goat's cheese mixture on top. Return to the oven for 7–8 minutes, or until the tops are bubbling and tinged with brown.

For the salad, rinse the rocket leaves and pat dry. Pour the olive oil and lemon juice into a bowl and season with plenty of salt and pepper. Add the rocket and toss gently to coat.

To serve, carefully remove the tarts from their tins and sit them in the centre of each serving plate. Spoon the red onion jam around the outside and top with the rocket salad.

Nanna's meat & barley soup

Whenever my sister and I were ill and had to be off school and Mummy was working, Nanna would come to look after us. I loved those 'not really that poorly' days under the duvet on the sofa with *Jackie* or *Girl* magazine and a bowl of Nanna's soup! Nanna would make everything 'OK' – she would tidy our (always) messy house and tell us stories of when she was little. Nanna nearly always made this soup from leftovers from a roast. So whatever meat they'd had would be put into it, bones and all, and barley added just before serving. As she got older and there was just herself to cook for, she would add a chop to the water along with the vegetables. I find that although this does add to the flavour it also needs a good bit of stock to enhance it. Feel free to play around with this 'wartime' soup recipe – there is no right or wrong, any vegetables and any meat go!

Serves 4–6

olive oil, for frying

1 onion, chopped

1–2 lamb chops (or a chicken leg) (optional) or any leftover shredded meat of your choice

2 carrots, chopped

2 medium potatoes, peeled and chopped

3 celery sticks, chopped

1.2 litres (2 pints) good-quality chicken or beef stock

100 g (3½ oz) pearl barley

100 g (3½ oz) green beans, chopped

freshly ground black pepper

Put a little oil in a heavy-based saucepan, add the onion and soften a little. Then add the chop, if using, vegetables and stock. Bring to the boil, turn the heat down and simmer over a low heat for about 1 hour (the longer you leave this the better it gets!).

About 20 minutes before serving, bring the soup back to the boil and add the barley and green beans. Take out the chops, if used, and shred the meat and return it to the soup. Add the shredded leftover meat at this point if using.

Serve in big soup bowls with a good grind of black pepper.

Brussels sprouts *with chestnuts & pancetta*

The only time I seem to eat sprouts is at Christmas. I know a lot of people have memories of 'soggy' sprouts but my mum's were always beautiful. We often had them with bacon and onion but I've 'doctored' it and replaced the bacon with pancetta and added chestnuts.

Serves 6 as a side dish

600 g (1 lb 2 oz) Brussels sprouts, trimmed and a cross cut in the base of each one

150 g (5 oz) pancetta, cubed

200 g (7 oz) vacuum-packed cooked chestnuts

25 g (1 oz) unsalted butter

Place the sprouts in a saucepan of boiling water and cook for 3 minutes until tender, but not too soft. Drain.

Heat a large frying pan, add the pancetta cubes and cook for a few minutes until softened.

Add the chestnuts, drained Brussels sprouts and butter and sauté for 4–5 minutes until the pancetta is crispy and the sprouts are slightly caramelised. Serve immediately.

Cauliflower gratin

This really is just a posh cauliflower cheese, really rich, made with cream and prosciutto.

Serves 4–6 as a side dish

1 large cauliflower, cut into florets

50 g (2 oz) butter

4 garlic cloves, crushed

125 g (4 oz) prosciutto, sliced thinly

2 tablespoons plain flour

175 ml (6 fl oz) milk

175 ml (6 fl oz) double cream

250 g (8 oz) Gruyére, grated

a pinch of cayenne pepper

50 g (2 oz) breadcrumbs (fresh or dried)

2 tablespoons freshly chopped flat-leaf parsley

freshly ground black pepper

Preheat the oven to 190°C (375°F), gas mark 5.

Blanch the cauliflower in a saucepan of boiling water for a few minutes, then drain.

Melt the butter in a large frying pan and add the garlic and prosciutto and sauté for about 2–3 minutes. Add the drained cauliflower, then stir in the flour, milk, cream, cheese and the cayenne pepper and season to taste. Bring to the boil.

Pour the cauliflower mixture into a shallow ovenproof dish and top with the breadcrumbs and the parsley. Cook in the preheated oven for about 30 minutes until crispy and golden on top.

Julie's chicken liver pâté

If I were playing a word/food association game about my mum, Chicken Liver Pâté would be in the top three! She was famous for her pâté; she made it at Christmas, for dinner parties and any other special occasions. I loved Christmas Day tea because of the Chicken Liver Pâté and melba toast. I remember watching Mummy light the pan when the brandy had been poured in and thinking it was a magic trick! The taste and smell of this pâté always brings back memories of Mummy making loads of extra melba toast and letting my sister and I use her special knives with the ceramic fruit handles to spread it.

Serves 6

425 g (14 oz) butter, softened

1 tablespoon olive oil

1 onion, chopped

2 garlic cloves, chopped

125 g (4 oz) streaky bacon, chopped

500 g (1 lb) chicken livers

1 wine glass of brandy, about 125 ml (4 fl oz)

1 tablespoon finely chopped tarragon

salt and freshly ground black pepper

fresh sage leaves, to finish (optional)

melba toast, to serve (optional)

Preheat the oven to 110°C (225°F), gas mark ¼.

Melt 175 g (6 oz) of the butter in a heatproof glass bowl in the preheated oven until it has separated. Strain off the clarified butter that will have risen to the top and set aside (you can also do this over a very low heat on the hob if you want to) and then discard the cloudy substance at the bottom.

Heat a large frying pan over a medium heat, add the oil and fry the onion, garlic and bacon until softened. Add the chicken livers and cook until they are slightly browned, but still soft. Don't overcook or the livers will become rubbery.

Pour in the brandy and light it to burn a little of the alcohol off. Do not let the flame burn too long, just blow it out once it's caught fire for a few seconds. Cook for a further minute.

Transfer the mixture to a food processor or blender and blitz until smooth. With the motor running, add the remaining butter and season to taste.

Pass the smooth mixture through a sieve, add the tarragon and spoon into 6 individual pots or ramekin dishes. Finish with sage leaves, if using, and top with the clarified butter (which will act as a seal). Leave to set in a cool place for at least 1 hour. Serve with melba toasts, if liked.

My mum never sieved the mixture, but I like the pâté smoother

Smoked salmon pâté

This was always another favourite for Christmas Day or Boxing Day tea. My mum had a fish mould that she used to serve it in, which I have done at times when I've wanted to recreate that 80s feeling! It's super-easy and can be whipped up in minutes.

Serves 4

200 g (7 oz) smoked salmon, cut into pieces

50 g (2 oz) unsalted butter, softened

1–2 tablespoons lemon juice

4 tablespoons double cream

a pinch of cayenne pepper

a small handful of freshly chopped chives

salt and freshly ground black pepper

melba toast, to serve

Put the smoked salmon pieces and the butter in a food processor or blender and blitz until smooth.

Add the lemon juice to taste, followed by the cream, cayenne pepper and chives.

Check the seasoning and divide the pâté between 4 ramekin dishes. Cover with cling film and chill in the fridge for at least 30 minutes to firm.

Serve with melba toast.

Posh fish pie

Fish pie is the ultimate comfort food. We had different versions growing up. I remember my mum's always had prawns in, but I think her sauce was quite cheesy and she did a potato topping. I decided to 'posh it up' one night when making dinner for my friends and the resulting recipe looks great – a bowl of beautiful fish in a creamy sauce topped with pastry. I demonstrated this dish at the MasterChef Live show.

Serves 4

butter, for greasing

1 x 375 g packet all butter ready-rolled puff pastry

flour, for dusting

1 egg, beaten

2 shallots, finely chopped

250 ml (8 fl oz) white wine

250 ml (8 fl oz) double cream

1 teaspoon Dijon or wholegrain mustard

1 x salmon fillet, weighing about 300 g (10 oz), skinned and chopped into pieces

1 x small monkfish tail fillet, weighing about 300 g (10 oz), chopped into pieces

1 x smoked haddock fillet, weighing about 300 g (10 oz), skinned and chopped into pieces

12 raw peeled king prawns

1 tablespoon freshly chopped parsley

1 tablespoon freshly chopped tarragon

salt and freshly ground black pepper

Preheat the oven to 200°C (400°F), gas mark 6 and grease a baking tray.

Lay the pastry out on a lightly floured worksurface and cut into four 11 cm (4½ inch) rounds. Brush with the beaten egg, place on the prepared baking tray and bake in the preheated oven for 20 minutes until puffed and golden.

Put the shallots and wine in a saucepan, bring to the boil and continue to boil until the liquid has reduced by half. Add the cream and let it bubble away until it is thick enough to coat the back of a spoon.

Stir in the mustard, chopped fish and the prawns, add some salt and pepper to taste and cook for about 5 minutes until the fish is cooked through and the prawns have turned pink. Stir through the parsley and tarragon.

Spoon the fish mixture into serving bowls and top with the cooked pastry discs to finish.

Pan-fried scallops
with chestnut soup & crispy sage leaves

I was asked to demo a Christmassy starter at one of the Good Food Shows. I started this dish as scallops with a chestnut purée but the purée was so delicious I decided to 'let it down', add some stock and make it into a soup with the scallops placed on top.

Serves 4

olive oil, for rubbing

12 scallops

25 g (1 oz) butter

For the soup

25 g (1 oz) butter

2 bacon rashers, chopped

2 shallots, finely chopped

2 tablespoons Cognac

1 x 200 g pack vacuum-packed chestnuts

500 ml (17 fl oz) chicken stock

50 ml (2 fl oz) double cream

salt and freshly ground black pepper

To finish

1 tablespoon olive oil

4 sage leaves

1 tablespoon cranberry jelly (optional)

To make the soup, melt the butter in a saucepan, add the bacon and shallots and cook over a medium heat until softened.

Add the Cognac, let it catch light so that the alcohol burns off a little, then add the chestnuts and stock and bring to the boil. Simmer for 5–10 minutes. Transfer to a food processor or blender and blitz until smooth.

Pour the smooth mixture back into the saucepan, stir in the cream and season to taste.

For the fried sage leaves, heat the oil in a frying pan and add the sage leaves. Cook until crisp, but be careful as they burn very quickly. Remove the sage leaves from the pan, blot on kitchen paper and then set aside.

To cook the scallops, heat a large frying pan. Season the scallops with salt and pepper and rub with olive oil. When the pan is piping hot, add the scallops and cook for about 1 minute. Turn them and add the butter. Cook for 1 minute, basting with the bubbling butter.

Pour the soup into shallow bowls, stack the scallops in the middle and top with a fried sage leaf.

As an optional garnish for special occasions, melt the cranberry jelly and put it in a chef's squeezy bottle. Dot very small blobs of the cranberry jelly onto the fried sage leaves. Serve immediately.

Glazed baked gammon

As I've said before I loved 'Christmas tea' – the table laden, for the second time that day, with all sorts of amazing food. My mum made the gammon on Christmas Eve and the smell of it cooking would fill the whole house. I use quite a large gammon here so there is aways plenty for leftovers!

Serves about 10–12

1 x unsmoked gammon joint, weighing about 4 kg (8 lb)

1 carrot, cut in half

1 onion, cut in half at root

1 celery stick

1 bay leaf

7 peppercorns

For the glaze

8 tablespoons marmalade (see page 194)

2 tablespoons wholegrain mustard

2 tablespoons black treacle

8–10 cloves

I usually soak the gammon in water overnight, but ask your butcher if this is necessary, and, if you do, discard the soaking water before starting.

Place the gammon in a large saucepan, cover with water and add the carrot, onion, celery, bay leaf and peppercorns. Bring to the boil and then turn down to a low simmer, covered, for 2¾ hours.

Preheat the oven to 180°C (350°F), gas mark 4.

When the gammon is cooked, make the glaze by mixing all of the ingredients (except the cloves) together in a bowl.

Remove the gammon from its cooking water and drain well. Cut the rind and some of fat off the gammon (leaving a thin layer of fat). Score the fat diagonally in a criss-cross pattern and then stud with the cloves all over. Put the gammon joint in a roasting tin, brush over the glaze and bake in the preheated oven for about 25–30 minutes until sticky and golden. Serve hot or cold.

After sandwiches for tea we would eat the gammon on Boxing Day with jacket potatoes or bubble and squeak. It is also great with my Piccalilli.

Potted ham rillettes *with soda bread*

I love these buttery pots! Easy to make using any leftover gammon, they make a great starter or a nice light tea! Serve with homemade Soda Bread (see below).

Makes 6

250 g (8 oz) cooked shredded gammon or ham hocks

300 g (10 oz) unsalted butter

2 pinches of freshly grated nutmeg

2–3 pinches of ground mace

3 pinches of cayenne pepper

3 fresh thyme sprigs, leaves only

For the soda bread

175 g (6 oz) plain flour, plus extra for dusting

175 g (6 oz) self-raising wholemeal flour

½ teaspoon bicarbonate of soda

½ teaspoon salt

300 ml (½ pint) natural yogurt

First, make the soda bread. Preheat the oven to 200°C (400°F), gas mark 6.

Mix the flours, bicarbonate of soda and salt together in a large mixing bowl. Make a well in the centre of the flour, add the yogurt and mix together.

Turn out onto a floured worksurface and knead gently for 3–4 minutes until smooth. Form into a round dough shape, cut a cross in the centre and place on a floured baking tray. Bake in the preheated oven for 25–30 minutes. You will know it's ready when you tap the bottom of the bread and it sounds hollow.

Meanwhile, make the ham rillettes. Divide the shredded ham between 6 ramekin dishes.

In a small saucepan, slowly melt the butter with the spices and thyme leaves. Pour this evenly into the ramekin dishes until the ham is just covered but still poking out. Cover and chill for 20 minutes until set. Remove from the fridge 20 minutes before serving and serve with the soda bread.

Slow-roasted pork belly

This is a great Sunday lunch recipe – pork belly is a delicious cut of meat and also very inexpensive. This method of scoring and cooking the pork belly is a great way to ensure the meat stays moist while getting that perfect crispy crackling. The water in the roasting tin sort of steams the meat while it roasts, while at the same time infusing the meat with all those lovely herbs.

Serves 6

1 x boned pork belly, weighing about 2 kg (4 lb)

For the rub

3 fresh thyme sprigs, leaves only

3 sage leaves, chopped

1 large garlic clove

1 teaspoon fennel seeds

4 teaspoons sea salt

For the roasting tin

750 ml (1¼ pints) water

2–3 fresh thyme sprigs

3 fresh sage leaves

3 garlic cloves

1 large teaspoon fennel seeds

Preheat the oven to 190°C (375°F), gas mark 5 and prepare the pork belly by scoring the skin diagonally 1 cm (½ inch) apart in a criss-cross pattern.

With a pestle and mortar, grind together all the ingredients for the rub. Pat off any moisture from the pork belly skin with kitchen paper and rub the ground mixture all over the skin. Add a little extra sea salt and place the meat on a wire rack.

Fill a roasting tin with the water and herbs and garlic and position the meat on a wire rack set over the top.

Bake in the preheated oven for 30 minutes. Turn the heat down to 150°C (300°F), gas mark 2 and cook for a further 1½ hours, topping up the roasting tin with water if it runs dry. Check the crackling – if it isn't crispy enough turn the heat back up to 200°C (400°F), gas mark 6 and roast it for another 20 minutes at the end.

Roast chicken with crème fraîche & herbs

The thing about this dish is that it's very little hassle with a very impressive sauce. Every time I make it my husband practically licks the plate clean!

Serves 6

300 ml (½ pint) crème fraîche

1 tablespoon freshly chopped tarragon

1 tablespoon freshly chopped flat-leaf parsley

1 garlic clove, finely chopped

juice of ½ lemon

1 x whole chicken, weighing about 2 kg (4 lb)

olive oil, for rubbing

150 ml (¼ pint) white wine

salt and freshly ground black pepper

Preheat the oven to 190°C (375°F), gas mark 5.

Mix the crème fraîche, herbs, garlic, lemon juice and some salt and pepper in a mixing bowl. Spoon the mixture into the cavity of the chicken (making sure the giblets have been removed).

Rub the chicken with olive oil and season, then bake in the preheated oven for about 1 hour 40 minutes, gently basting with the oil but taking care to keep the sauce inside the chicken.

Test to see if the chicken is cooked by piercing the flesh at the leg joint with a sharp knife, pressing down gently – if clear juices run out it should be done. Transfer the chicken to a board to rest and spoon out the sauce from the cavity into the roasting tin.

Put the roasting tin over a medium heat on the hob, add the wine and bring to the boil. Whisk until the sauce comes together, then serve spooned over the carved chicken.

You could tie the chicken legs together to keep the sauce in the cavity – you would then need to pour the filling out into the roasting pan to finish the sauce.

Pan-fried chicken
with bubble & squeak potato cakes

This is a really good way of using up any leftover potatoes and vegetables. It's so simple to make and has the added bonus of tasting great!

Serves 4

4 x boneless chicken breasts, weighing about 200 g (7 oz) each, skin on (or 2 thighs or legs per person)

olive oil, for rubbing and frying

a few fresh thyme sprigs

100 g (3½ oz) pancetta, cubed

3–4 leeks, trimmed and sliced

a knob of butter

4 large potatoes, boiled and mashed

flour, for dusting

salt and freshly ground black pepper

Preheat the oven to 200°C (400°F), gas mark 6. Rub the chicken breasts all over with olive oil and season.

Heat an ovenproof frying pan and put the chicken in, skin side down, to brown for about 5 minutes. Turn over and brown on the other side for 2 minutes, then add a couple of thyme sprigs. Transfer the pan to the preheated oven and cook for about 10–15 minutes, or until cooked through.

Meanwhile, in a smaller frying pan, cook the pancetta for about 2–3 minutes. Add the leeks and cook until softened. Add the leaves from a few more thyme sprigs and a little olive oil if needed, then finish off with a knob of butter.

Mix the pancetta and leeks into the mashed potato and season. Shape into patties and dust in flour.

Heat a frying pan with a little olive oil and cook the bubble and squeak patties for about 5 minutes on each side until brown and crispy. Transfer them to a plate and serve with the chicken sliced diagonally in half and resting on top.

Turkey & leek pie

I hate throwing things away – especially food. We always seem to have loads of turkey left after Christmas so here's a great leftover recipe. It also works just as well with chicken.

Serves 6

150 g (5 oz) pancetta or bacon, cubed

3–4 fresh thyme sprigs

1.5 kg (3 lb) leeks, trimmed and sliced

2 tablespoons olive oil

a knob of butter, plus extra for greasing

about 800 g (1 lb 10 oz) cold, cooked turkey breast meat or a mixture of brown and white meat (whatever you prefer or have left over)

50 g (2 oz) plain flour

1.2 litres (2 pints) chicken stock

50 ml (2 fl oz) double cream

1 x 375 g pack chilled ready-rolled puff pastry

1 egg, beaten

salt and freshly ground black pepper

Preheat the oven to 190°C (350°F), gas mark 5.

Heat a large, dry frying pan, add the pancetta or bacon cubes and thyme and cook over a medium to high heat for 3–4 minutes.

Add the leeks to the pan with the olive oil and a knob of butter. Reduce the heat to low and soften for about 15–20 minutes, stirring occasionally, so that the leeks don't stick.

Add the turkey to the pan and stir through. Mix in the flour and then pour over the stock. Stir until mixed and then add the cream and season to taste. Bring to the boil and then take the pan off the heat.

Using a slotted spoon, put the turkey and leek mixture into a large pie dish. If the 'gravy' is too runny for your liking continue to boil and reduce it for a few minutes longer until it thickens. Once the right consistency has been achieved, pour it over the pie filling in the dish.

Grease the rim of the pie dish and roll the puff pastry out to the right size to cover your pie dish. Lay the pastry over the top, pinch around the edges to seal and then brush with beaten egg. Bake in the preheated oven for 40 minutes until puffed and golden brown on top.

Duck with celeriac & cherries

My godmother, Pat, used to make duck with a cherry sauce that my mum loved. She says she never uses a recipe so I've made up my own version of her sauce and served it with celeriac chips. I think sauces can be difficult to make, especially red wine reductions. The difficulty, I think, is having the confidence to trust your instincts and keep it reducing until the last minute. It's knowing when to take it off the heat and whisk in the butter and it is trial and error, but trust me it is so worth it when you get it right. The first time I successfully made this sauce I jumped up and down, phoned all my friends and had a massive smile on my face for hours! I know, I know, it's only a sauce!

Serves 4

4 x duck breasts, weighing about 175 g (6 oz) each

salt and freshly ground black pepper

For the sauce

½ bottle (350 ml/12 fl oz) port

1 shallot, chopped

1 teaspoon grated orange rind

4 tablespoons butter, about 50 g (2 oz)

1 x 260 g tin pitted black cherries, drained

For the celeriac chips

2 medium celeriac

olive oil

sea salt

First, make the sauce. Put the port, shallot and orange rind into a saucepan and bring to the boil. When it has reduced by half strain the shallots, reserving the liquid, and then put the sauce back on the heat. Keep reducing it down so the mixture is thick and bubbly. You will know the sauce is reaching the correct thickness when the bubbles become noticeably bigger. Take it off the heat and whisk in the butter in 25 g (1 oz) blocks, so the sauce is thick and glossy. Add the drained cherries and warm through over a really low heat. Set aside until needed.

To make the celeriac chips, preheat the oven to 200°C (400°F), gas mark 6 and heat a roasting tin with a thin layer of olive oil. Peel the celeriac and cut it into thick slices, then into chunky chips. Bring a large saucepan of salted water to the boil, blanche the chips for 1–2 minutes, then drain. Take the tin out of the oven and toss the chips in the hot oil and season. Cook in the preheated oven for 25–30 minutes until crispy but tender. Alternatively, you could deep-fry the chips once they have been blanched.

Meanwhile, score the duck skin and season. Place the duck breasts, skin side down, in a cold ovenproof frying pan and put over a medium heat for about 6–7 minutes until the skin is crispy. Turn the duck over and cook for a further minute. Pour off the fat from the pan, then transfer to the oven for about 6–8 minutes, depending on the size of the duck breast.

Sprinkle the celeriac chips with sea salt, reheat the sauce if necessary and serve it with the duck breasts and celeriac chips.

Mummy's toad in the hole

This was a real family favourite in our house when I was growing up and still is now. When making the sausage patties my mum used to keep a bowl of cold water next to her to dip her hands in before shaping them. It makes it a lot easier.

Serves 3–4

500 g (1 lb) sausagemeat

1 shallot, finely chopped

1 apple, peeled and grated

4 streaky bacon rashers, chopped

1 tablespoon freshly chopped sage

1 garlic clove, finely chopped

90 ml (3½ fl oz) olive oil

salt and freshly ground black pepper

onion gravy, to serve (optional)

For the batter

175 g (6 oz) plain flour (I always sieve it twice)

2 teaspoons mustard powder

4 eggs

450 ml (¾ pint) whole milk

Preheat the oven to 180°C (350°F), gas mark 4.

First, make the batter: In a bowl, mix the flour, mustard powder and some salt and pepper. Whisk the eggs into the milk in a separate bowl. Make a well in the centre of the flour mixture and pour in the egg/milk mixture. Beat until mixed and set aside.

Mix the sausagemeat, shallot, grated apple, bacon, sage, garlic and some salt and pepper together in a large bowl. Shape into 9 little patties.

Heat 15 ml (1 teaspoon) of the olive oil in a frying pan and fry the patties for 3–4 minutes until just browned, turning over as and when needed.

Pour the remaining olive oil into a 3.6 litres (6 pint) ovenproof dish and put it in the preheated oven for about 7–10 minutes until the oil is smoking hot. Add the browned patties and pour over the batter. Put the dish back in the oven for 40 minutes until puffed up and golden brown and the batter surrounding the patties has set. Serve with onion gravy, if liked.

Mince 3 ways

I nearly didn't include this because it's just a basic mince stew, but it was such a staple in our house growing up and it's such comfort food that I felt I had to. There were times when we were growing up when money was tight. I remember my mum talking about having no money and making such statements as 'Right. That's it, we're going on an economy drive. We're just going to eat mince!' We loved this stew with dumplings, or she would make it into cottage pie, or a pastry plate pie, which was also Nanna's forte! It's great if you make a big batch of mince stew and freeze it so that when it comes to cooking you can just defrost it and add dumplings, potatoes or pastry.

All dishes serves 4

For the mince stew

500 g (1 lb) lean minced beef

1 onion, finely chopped

1 leek, finely chopped

about 2–3 carrots, finely diced

about 2 celery sticks, finely chopped

6 mushrooms, finely chopped

1 large teaspoon Marmite

500 ml (17 fl oz) beef stock

salt and freshly ground black pepper

For the dumplings (makes 8)

125 g (4 oz) self-raising flour

50 g (2 oz) suet

2 fresh thyme sprigs, leaves only

5 tablespoons water

salt

For the cottage pie topping

1 kg (2 lb) potatoes, peeled and chopped

125 g (4 oz) butter

salt and freshly ground black pepper

First, make the mince stew. Brown the mince in a large frying pan over a medium heat. Add the onion, leek, carrots, celery and mushrooms and fry for about 5 minutes.

Add the Marmite and stock, bring to the boil and then turn the heat down to a low simmer and cook for at least 45 minutes. Season to taste (depending on what beef stock you use, you may need to add extra for taste).

Now, either freeze in batches for later use or make up into one of the following dishes:

For the mince stew and dumplings: mix all of the dumpling ingredients together in a bowl until it comes together in a sticky dough. Roll the dumplings into balls and place them on top of the simmering mince stew. Let it bubble away with a lid on for about 20 minutes.

For the cottage pie: continue to boil and reduce the mince stew a little (or drain some liquid off) so that it's not swimming in gravy. Preheat the oven to 180°C (350°F), gas mark 4. Put the potatoes in a large saucepan of cold water. Bring to the boil, turn the heat down and simmer for 20 minutes. Take off the heat and drain. Return the potatoes to the pan, add the butter, season and mash well. Transfer the mince to an ovenproof dish, let it cool a little and then top with the mashed potato. Bake in the preheated oven for 30–40 minutes until the topping is lightly golden and crisp.

For the pastry plate pie topping

375 g (12 oz) plain flour, plus extra for dusting

125 g (4 oz) cold lard, cubed

50 g (2 oz) cold margarine or butter, cubed

1 tablespoon water

1 egg, beaten

a pinch of salt

For the pastry plate pie: Make the pastry (see page 39) and rest in the fridge for 30 minutes. Preheat the oven to 180°C (350°F), gas mark 4. Cut the pastry in half and roll out on a lightly floured worksurface into 2 discs – one the size of the pie plate and the other slightly larger. Put the smaller disc on the bottom of the pie plate, use a slotted spoon to add the mince stew (reserving the juice). Then top with the slightly larger pastry disc and prick the middle with a fork. Brush the pastry top with the beaten egg and cook in the preheated oven for about 30–40 minutes until golden on top. Use the reserved juice to make a gravy to serve with the pie, if liked.

Beef stroganoff

This is a real 80s favourite! My mum used to make it a lot for dinner parties and I've revived it for family and friends. She always used fresh mushrooms, but one day I didn't have any and ended up using dry porcini mushrooms that really added a lovely flavour.

Serves 4

50 g (2 oz) unsalted butter

1 onion, finely sliced

1 teaspoon paprika (smoked if you have it)

25 g (1 oz) dried porcini mushrooms (covered in boiling water and left to soak for 30 minutes)

700 g (1 lb 6 oz) beef fillet, cut into 1 cm (½ inch) strips

300 ml (½ pint) soured cream

1 dessertspoon Dijon mustard

a squeeze of lemon juice

50 ml (2 fl oz) double cream

a handful of freshly chopped flat-leaf parsley

oil, for frying

salt and freshly ground black pepper

greens, rice or lyonnaise potatoes, to serve

Heat the butter in a large frying pan and sauté the onion and paprika slowly until softened.

Drain the mushrooms (reserving the liquid), chop roughly, then add to the pan and cook for 3 minutes. Use a slotted spoon to transfer to a plate and set aside.

Add a little extra oil, if needed, to the frying pan and seal the beef in batches. Use a slotted spoon to transfer the meat to a plate.

Return the onion mixture to the pan, add the soured cream and 100 ml (3½ fl oz) of the reserved mushroom soaking liquid and cook for 2–3 minutes. Stir in the Dijon mustard, lemon juice and season with salt and pepper.

Return the sealed beef to the pan and heat through gently for about 3–5 minutes until just cooked through.

Just before serving, stir in the cream and the chopped parsley. Serve with greens, rice or lyonnaise potatoes.

Nannie's nut roast

My great-grandmother 'Nannie' was Seventh Day Adventist, which meant she was extremely religious and also a vegetarian. She was very frugal, she didn't drink alcohol or caffeine and lived to the ripe old age of 92. I remember Nannie always baked her own wholemeal bread, had the shiniest false teeth I'd ever seen and made a mean nut roast. Nannie's Nut Roast is quick and easy and is a real Faulkner family favourite.

Serves 4

25 g (1 oz) butter, plus extra for greasing

1 onion, chopped

200 g (7 oz) mixed chopped nuts

100 g (3½ oz) fresh breadcrumbs

200 g (7 oz) Cheddar cheese, grated

1 teaspoon Marmite

Preheat the oven to 180°C (350°F), gas mark 4 and grease a 1 kg (2 lb) loaf tin.

Melt the butter in a large frying pan and gently fry the onion until softened. Take off the heat and add the nuts, breadcrumbs, cheese, Marmite and 1 tablespoon water and combine. Put the mixture in the loaf tin and bake in the preheated oven for 25 minutes.

Note: I have put 1 tablespoon water as a guide. My dad prefers it drier and uses very little; my sister and I use a bit more.

Nina's bread sauce

My godmother, Nina, comes for Christmas every other year and we love having her and her husband, Andrew. Among many fantastic recipes she makes this gorgeous bread sauce.

Serves 8

1 onion, peeled

7 cloves

425 ml (14½ fl oz) milk

6 black peppercorns

1 bay leaf

75 g (3 oz) fresh breadcrumbs

50 g (2 oz) butter

2 tablespoons double cream

salt and freshly ground black pepper

Cut the onion in half and stud the cloves into both halves. Put the onion in a saucepan with the milk, peppercorns, bay leaf and a pinch of salt. Bring to the boil, take off the heat and leave to infuse for at least 2 hours.

Strain the sauce, put the onion aside and return the infused milk to the pan. Stir the breadcrumbs into the milk, add half the butter and cook until the sauce is thickened.

Take half the reserved onion, remove the cloves and liquidise in a food processor or blender. Add this purée to the sauce in the pan along with the rest of the butter and the cream. Add salt and pepper to taste and heat through. Best eaten within 3–4 days.

Mince pies

My grandma Betty's mince pies to me were the first sign of Christmas. She was always so organised that her first batch was easily baked in late November with mincemeat she'd made the year before. What always amused me was that both grandmothers made their own mince pies, and both preferred the other's pastry! I loved both versions and my pastry comes out somewhere in between both of theirs. The mincemeat recipe below makes about 3 kg (6 lb) in total – you will not need all of it for the mince pies, so use some now and the rest will keep for many months and even years if mixed with more brandy when used.

Makes about 24

For the mincemeat

500 g (1 lb) currants

500 g (1 lb) raisins

500 g (1 lb) peeled and cored cooking apples

1–2 tablespoons brandy

1 teaspoon mixed spice

½ teaspoon ground cinnamon

500 g (1 lb) sultanas

500 g (1 lb) soft brown sugar

500 g (1 lb) shredded suet

For the mince pies

375 g (12 oz) plain flour, plus extra for dusting

125 g (4 oz) cold lard, cubed

50 g (2 oz) cold margarine, cubed

a pinch of salt

1–2 tablespoons cold water

600 g (1 lb 2 oz) mincemeat

First, make the mincemeat. Preheat the oven to 160°C (325°F), gas mark 3. Put 7 clean jars on a baking tray and place in the oven to sterilise for at least 5 minutes.

Put the currants, raisins, apples, brandy, mixed spice and cinnamon in a food processor or blender and blitz until mixed, but still chunky. Put the sultanas, sugar and suet in a bowl and mix together. Add in the processed mixture and stir until mixed.

Spoon the mincemeat into the sterilised jars, leaving 1 cm (½ inch) 'breathing space' at the top. Cover with a waxed disc and a circle of cellophane before sealing. Put the jars in a dark, cool place to store until you are ready to make the mince pies.

To make the mince pies, preheat the oven to 180°C (350°F), gas mark 4 and lightly grease two 12-hole bun tins.

Put the flour, lard, margarine and salt in a food processor or blender and pulse until the mixture resembles fine breadcrumbs. Add the cold water and pulse again until a dough is formed. Shape in to a round dough, wrap in cling film and chill for 30 minutes before using.

Roll the pastry out on a lightly floured worksurface to about 5 mm (¼ inch) thick and use round cutters to cut out twenty-four 8 cm (3½ inch) circles and twenty-four 6–7 cm (2½–3 inch) circles. Place a bigger circle in the base of each hole of the bun tin, add a teaspoon of the mincemeat and then cover with the smaller circle. Wet the rim with water to seal it, then prick the tops with a fork. Bake in the preheated oven for 25–30 minutes.

Christmas biscuits

I have made these biscuits with Billie for the past few years and she loves cutting out the star shapes and decorating the biscuits. I admit I have to put them on the tree in batches because every morning there are little bites out of the reachable ones! Also, being biscuits, they will go soft, so decorate the tree with them on the days you want to eat them.

Makes 32

250 g (8 oz) unsalted butter, softened, plus extra for greasing

140 g (4½ oz) caster sugar

1 egg yolk

300 g (10 oz) plain flour, plus extra for dusting

1 teaspoon all-spice

1 teaspoon ground ginger

edible silver balls, to decorate (optional)

For the icing

100 g (3½ oz) icing sugar

1 tablespoon warm water

food colouring (optional)

Cream the butter and sugar together in a mixing bowl for around 5 minutes until pale and creamy. Mix in the egg yolk.

Sift the flour and spices together into a separate bowl and then fold this in to the creamed mixture until it comes together in a dough. Wrap the dough in cling film and chill for at least 2 hours.

Roll the dough out on a lightly floured worksurface to about 5 mm (¼ inch) thick. Use a 7 cm (3 inch) star-shaped cutter to cut out as many stars as you can manage, re-rolling the trimmings as needed.

Use a wooden skewer to make a little hole in one of the points of each star (this is to thread ribbon through so the biscuits can be hung when cooked).

Place onto 1–2 greased baking trays and chill in the fridge for 30 minutes – this stops the biscuits from spreading. Meanwhile, preheat the oven to 180°C (350°F), gas mark 4.

Bake the chilled biscuits in the preheated oven for 12 minutes. Cool on a wire rack.

While the biscuits are cooling, make the icing. Sieve the icing sugar into a bowl. Add the warm water gradually and mix until the icing coats the back of a spoon. Add a few drops of food colouring, if using, and stir in. Decorate as desired with icing and edible silver balls, if using, and hang with pretty ribbon. Store in an airtight container for 1–2 days only (they will quickly go soft).

I was talking to a friend the other day about Christmas and *how magical it is when you've got a child.*

Christmas sweet box

This is a lovely gift anytime of year and makes a change from giving a bottle of wine at a dinner party. When I was going through the madness of IVF I made loads of these to give to my wonderful friends who all supported me through a pretty tough couple of years.

The fudge is delicious. You can play around with flavours, putting different nuts or fruit in, but it's just as lovely plain. I think the key to making good fudge is to very slowly melt the sugar in the pan first so it is properly dissolved. And make sure you beat it well, too.

Makes enough for about 5 mixed gift boxes of sweets

For the rich chocolate truffles and liqueur truffles (makes about 10 each)

200 g (7 oz) dark chocolate

25 g (1 oz) butter

200 ml (7 fl oz) double cream

1–2 tablespoons cream liqueur

cocoa powder, for dusting

For the honeycomb (makes about 24 pieces)

oil, for greasing

4 tablespoons golden syrup

200 g (7 oz) caster sugar

1 tablespoon bicarbonate of soda

To make the rich chocolate truffles and liqueur truffles:

Chop the chocolate in a food processor or blender until gravel-like, then tip into a large mixing bowl.

Gently heat the butter and cream together in a saucepan, but don't let it boil. Pour the heated butter and cream into the chocolate and stir until glossy. Divide the mixture in half and stir the liqueur into one half of the mixture.

With a melon-baller (if you have one or you can shape them with a teaspoon), shape into balls and dust with cocoa powder. Chill in the fridge for 1–2 hours.

To make the honeycomb:

Line a 20 cm (8 inch) square cake tin with non-stick baking paper and grease or spray with oil.

In a large saucepan, gently heat the golden syrup and caster sugar together until the sugar has melted. Increase the heat and simmer for a further 4–5 minutes until the mixture has thickened and is a darker caramel colour.

Take the pan off the heat and quickly whisk in the bicarbonate of soda – the mixture will froth up quite a lot. Pour into the prepared tin and leave to set. This should take a minimum of 30 minutes. Break into pieces to serve.

For the vanilla, almond & cranberry fudge (makes about 40 pieces)

1 x 397 g can condensed milk

500 g (1 lb) granulated sugar

125 ml (4 fl oz) water

50 g (2 oz) butter

1 vanilla pod, split lengthways or 1 teaspoon vanilla extract

40 g (1½ oz) blanched almonds, chopped

40g (1½ oz) dried cranberries, chopped

For the peppermint creams (makes about 40 pieces)

500 g (1 lb) icing sugar, plus extra for dusting

1 egg white

juice of ½ lemon

½ teaspoon peppermint extract

food colouring (optional)

200 g (7 oz) good-quality dark chocolate, broken into pieces

To make the vanilla, almond and cranberry fudge:

Line and grease a 20 cm (8 inch) square cake tin. Put the condensed milk, sugar, water, butter and vanilla seeds from the split pod or extract into a heavy-based saucepan and cook over a very low heat for about 10 minutes until the sugar is properly dissolved, stirring all the time.

Once the sugar is dissolved, turn up the heat and boil for about 7–10 minutes, stirring occasionally. The mixture should bubble the whole time but make sure it doesn't burn. After 7 minutes, drop a little of the mixture into cold water – if it forms a soft ball when rolled between your fingers and thumb it is ready. Take off the heat and put the pan on a cold surface for 3–4 minutes.

Tip the nuts and cranberries into the mixture and beat well – don't skip this stage as the beating is very important for the consistency of the fudge. Pour into the prepared tin and leave to set for about 3–4 hours.

To make the peppermint creams:

Sieve the icing sugar into a bowl. Add the egg white and mix together. Lightly dust the worksurface with icing sugar and knead this mixture with your hands until the egg white and sugar are blended together – this mixture needs to be pliable so you may need to add the lemon juice a little at a time.

Add the peppermint extract and food colouring, if using. Knead again until mixed and taste.

Lightly dust the work surface with icing sugar again and roll out onto a cold, flat surface and cut into small circles, ovals or diamonds.

Melt the chocolate in a bowl set over a saucepan of simmering water, making sure the base of the bowl does not touch the water. Dip half of each cream shape into the dark chocolate and leave on a lined or non-stick baking tray to set.

...be aware that it's going
to crack when rolled – it is
supposed to happen, but just
be gentle. Enjoy!

Chocolate roulade

One of my favourites of Mummy's puddings was her chocolate roulade. It was light, rich, gooey and chewy all at the same time! I remember her whipping them up at a moment's notice, usually with the phone attached to her ear, chatting to one of her friends and making it look so easy. It tastes great the following day, even chewier, as my sister and I would devour any remains for breakfast! I, however, found about three chocolate roulade recipes in my mum's books, each one slightly different to the other. I tried all of them, and it was, of course, the last one I tried that was 'The One'. Actually, it really isn't difficult, just don't 'over-mix' the chocolate into the egg whites.

Serves 6

175 g (6 oz) dark chocolate, broken into pieces

4 eggs

175 g (6 oz) caster sugar

icing sugar, for dusting

200–300 ml (7–10 fl oz) double cream

Preheat the oven to 180°C (350°F), gas mark 4. Line a 34 x 23 cm (13 x 9 inch) Swiss roll tin with greaseproof paper.

Melt the chocolate in a bowl set over a saucepan of simmering water, making sure the base of the bowl does not touch the water.

Separate the eggs, setting aside the whites. Beat the yolks and sugar together in a mixing bowl until pale and creamy. Add the melted chocolate and beat until incorporated.

In a separate bowl, whisk the egg whites, either by hand or with a hand-held electric mixer, for 1–2 minutes until they are stiff, but not dry. Fold this into the chocolate mixture one-third at a time until just combined – do not over-mix.

Pour the cake mixture into the prepared tin and bake in the preheated oven for 15–20 minutes. Leave the cake to cool in the tin, covered with foil, for 3–4 hours or overnight.

Remove the foil from the tin, lie the foil flat on the worksurface and sprinkle it with icing sugar. Turn the cake out onto the foil so that the crispy top is on the bottom being coated with the icing sugar. Loosen the paper lining and gently peel off the cake.

Whip the cream in a mixing bowl, either by hand or with a hand-held electric mixer, and spread it over the cake.

Use the foil to help carefully roll the cake over into a Swiss roll. Cut into slices to serve.

Individual sticky toffee puddings

I made these for Boxing Day lunch a few years ago, because you can make them in advance, freeze and then finish them off on the day. Everyone thought they looked so pretty and said that I'd made such an effort but really it was so easy. They are beautifully light and I always end up making double the sauce because it's delicious and I like my pudding swimming in it!

Makes 8

175 g (6 oz) pitted dates, chopped

300 ml (½ pint) boiling water

1 teaspoon bicarbonate of soda

50 g (2 oz) unsalted butter, softened, plus extra for greasing

175 g (6 oz) unrefined caster sugar

2 eggs, beaten

210 g (7 oz) self-raising flour, sifted

1 vanilla pod, split lengthways

chopped walnuts, to finish

double cream, to serve (optional)

For the sauce

250 g (8 oz) unsalted butter

300 g (10 oz) soft brown sugar

400 ml (14 fl oz) single cream

Preheat the oven to 180°C (350°F), gas mark 4. Grease eight 200 ml (7 fl oz) mini pudding basins or ramekin dishes and line each base with a small circle of greaseproof paper (this is time consuming but vital if you want to turn the puddings out intact!).

Put the dates along with the boiling water and bicarbonate of soda into a bowl and put to one side. In another bowl, cream the butter and sugar together until light and fluffy.

Add the eggs a little at a time, mixing well between each addition. Fold in the flour, followed by the dates and their soaking liquid. Scrape the seeds from the split vanilla pod into the bowl and mix well. You will have a wet mixture but don't be worried as this is how it is meant to be.

Divide this mixture between the moulds, taking care not to fill them more than two-thirds full. Place the moulds or ramekin dishes on a baking tray and bake in the preheated oven for about 25 minutes, or until a metal skewer comes out clean when tested.

While the puddings are cooking, make the sauce. Put all the sauce ingredients into a saucepan, bring to the boil and simmer for 5 minutes, stirring from time to time.

When the puddings are cooked, turn them out onto a clean, lined baking tray and spoon over half of the sauce. Return to the oven for 5 minutes. Serve the puddings with the remaining sauce, some chopped walnuts and double cream.

Note: these puddings can be frozen in their moulds, covered with cling film, after they are cooked and cooled. Defrost, then heat for about 10 minutes in an oven preheated to 180°C (350°F), gas mark 4. The sauce can be made when you are ready to serve them.

Nina's chocolate mousse

Another classic from my godmother, Nina. These mousses are really easy, but don't be tempted to use too rich a chocolate or they won't work! I would normally use a good-quality chocolate with a high percentage of cocoa solids for these kind of desserts, but this one really does work better with a standard chocolate. My nieces love them, as does Billie, and they freeze beautifully, making them an easy make-ahead dessert.

Makes 10

300 g (10 oz) dark chocolate, broken into pieces

3 tablespoons water

6 eggs, separated

Melt the chocolate and the water in a bowl set over a saucepan of simmering water, making sure the base of the bowl does not touch the water.

Whisk the egg whites, either by hand or with a hand-held electric mixer, in a large clean bowl, until they form stiff peaks.

Allow the chocolate to cool a little and then whisk in the yolks one at a time. Mix until well combined. Fold in the egg whites, taking care not to knock all the air out.

Divide the mixture between 10 ramekin dishes or little cups and chill for at least 3 hours before serving.

Note: These can be made in advance and stored, covered, in the freezer for up to 1 month.

Christmas cake

I was talking to a friend the other day about Christmas, how magical it is when you've got a child. You try to cling on to it as a teenager and then you're in a sort of 'no man's land' until you're grown up enough to make Christmas into what you want it to be. Having my daughter made me want to recreate the wonderful Christmas times from my childhood, and we now always honour the traditions we used to follow.

My mum loved Christmas, especially all the preparation and all the food that went with it. She loved a list (as do I!) and I still have a few of hers in her precious handwriting.

My godmother, Pat, is the Christmas queen! We used to go round to her house for drinks on Christmas morning. She would have a Christmas doorbell, Christmas earrings, flashing badges, the whole works! Pat and Mummy shared the same Christmas cake recipe. They would make it about the first week of December, 'feed' it with brandy a week later and leave it wrapped in greaseproof paper until they had time to make the marzipan and royal icing. The icing was always rock hard and the marzipan deliciously creamy. I loved it so much, I asked Pat to recreate it for my wedding day. I had three square tiers of hard, smooth royal icing and wonderfully rich fruit cake. When we were little my sister and I would help my mum with the marzipan and with the leftovers we'd make holly berries and leaves and snowmen that we'd paint with food colouring.

I remember my sister and I being called into the kitchen to make a wish when my mum was mixing the Christmas cake and my godmother Pat still phones her now grown-up family, who have flown the nest, for them to wish along the phone lines!

As I'm not a fan of mixed peel I have substituted it with an extra 50 g (2 oz) cherries in the past, but I am giving you the cake recipe as Mummy and Pat intended. Feel free to play about with it and subsitute any ingredients with your favourites. For speed and ease I have used a 400 g block of ready-to-roll icing (rolled out to the thickness of a £1.00 coin), as this gives a really smooth finish. But once you've gone to the trouble of making your own cake and marzipan it's a real sense of achievement to ice your own cake.

Serves 10–12

For the cake

1 kg (2 lb) mixed dried fruit

125 g (4 oz) glacé cherries, halved

50 g (2 oz) ground almonds

50 g (2 oz) mixed peel

125 g (4 oz) raisins

300 g (10 oz) plain flour

1 teaspoon grated nutmeg

½ teaspoon mixed spice

½ teaspoon ground cinnamon

300 g (10 oz) soft margarine

300 g (10 oz) caster sugar

finely grated rind of 1 lemon

6 eggs

1–2 tablespoons brandy

For the marzipan

300 g (10 oz) ground almonds

125 g (4 oz) caster sugar

125 g (4 oz) icing sugar

2 small eggs

1 teaspoon lemon juice

¼ teaspoon vanilla extract

¼ teaspoon almond essence

For the royal icing

2 egg whites

¼ teaspoon glycerine

1 teaspoon lemon juice

500 g (1 lb) icing sugar, sieved

Preheat the oven to 150°C (300°F), gas mark 2 and line a 23 cm (9 inch) cake tin (any shape) with greaseproof paper (lining both top and sides).

Put the mixed dried fruit, cherries, ground almonds, mixed peel and raisins in a large mixing bowl.

In a separate bowl, put the flour, spices, margarine, caster sugar and lemon rind and beat everything together with a hand-held electric mixer or by hand with a wooden spoon. Add the eggs, beating in one at a time. Fold the mixed fruit into the flour in two batches. Add 1 teaspoon (or 2!) of the brandy and mix well. Pour into the prepared tin and level the surface.

Bake in the preheated oven for about 2 hours until the cake smells strongly. Test to see if it is cooked by piercing the top of the cake with a skewer in several places – it should come out clean without any mixture sticking to it. Leave to cool in the tin for 5–10 minutes and then turn out onto a wire rack.

Pierce again with a skewer in several places and sprinkle a capful of brandy over the top. Wrap in greaseproof paper and aluminium foil and store in an airtight container.

To make the marzipan, mix the almonds, sugar and icing sugar together in one bowl, and the eggs, lemon juice, vanilla extract and almond essence in another bowl. Add the wet ingredients to the dry and mix with a wooden spoon and then knead until it comes together in a smooth dough – it should only take a few minutes for the dough to become pliable. The consistency should be pastry-like. Add more icing sugar if necessary to bring the dough together. Wrap in cling film and store in an airtight container until you are ready to assemble your cake.

To make the royal icing, whisk the egg whites, either by hand or with a hand-held electric mixer, in a bowl until stiff (alternatively, use an electric mixer with the whisk attachment fitted). Add the glycerine and lemon juice and gradually beat in the icing sugar. Beat for 5 minutes. You may need to add more icing sugar depending on the size of the eggs to achieve a stiff consistency – peaks should stay upright when tested with your whisk.

Next, assemble the cake. If necessary, level the top of the cake – Mummy turned hers upside down. Melt the apricot jam

To assemble

100 g (3½ oz) apricot jam, for glazing

icing sugar, for dusting

in a bowl in the microwave on full power for 1 minute until smooth. Brush the sides of the cake with the melted apricot jam and liberally sprinkle the surface with icing sugar. Halve the marzipan and roll one half out into a thin strip, roughly the depth of the cake, on a lightly floured surface – this can be done in sections as joints will be covered by the icing. Roll and lift the mazipan onto the sides of the cake so that it is completely covered. Trim the top edge, but I usually tuck the bottom under the cake to help fill any gaps. Brush the top of the cake with apricot jam (it may need to be reheated in the microwave). Sprinkle the surface with icing sugar and roll out the rest of the marzipan into a circle the same size as the top of the cake. Lay the marzipan disc on top of the cake and smooth out with your hands. Leave to dry for 24 hours before icing.

Ice the cake. Place a large spoonful of icing in the centre of the cake and, with a palette knife, using a motion like spreading butter, smooth the icing over the surface of the cake, keeping the knife flat to eliminate any air bubbles. Leave to dry before coating the side/s of the cake. Leave to dry for 24 hours or more. Decorate as desired.

Note: I like to sprinkle with a capful of brandy once the cake has been wrapped and left for a week (called 'feeding' the cake), but if you haven't got time it doesn't matter. This cake can be made for any special occasion 4–6 weeks in advance but will still taste as good if it only has a few days to mature. If using ready-to-roll icing brush the marzipan with 50 ml (2 fl oz) brandy or vodka (using water can attract bacteria, which can cause fermentation between the layers of icing and marzipan).

Pat's brandy butter

A lovely accompaniment to Christmas pudding or cake, or a mince pie.

Makes 625 g (1¼ lb)

125 g (4 oz) unsalted butter, softened

500 g (1 lb) icing sugar

4 tablespoons brandy

Whisk the butter with one-third of the icing sugar in a bowl and then add the brandy. Whisk in the rest of the icing sugar, a spoon at a time. Cover and keep in the fridge for 3–5 days.

Index

Thank you – Without all of you this book couldn't and wouldn't have happened...

My godmothers Ann, Pat and Nina and Aunt Sue for the meetings and the memories and all your recipe tips and love and support.

To my sister Victoria, my reason, my constant, my lifeboat. For all your help typing out recipes, keeping things in order and being my little editor.

My Daddy, for your never-ending support, even though you will always have to look after me!!

Stacks for putting up with the all consuming nightmare I've become. I love you.

My Nanna, for your stories.

Angie, Jasee, Nic, Posh, Al, Em, my family, my circle that continues.

John T thank you so much for all your support, my friend, mentor, inspiration and devil killer.

Everybody at Smiths, Michael and the Topfloor boys, the wine rooms for letting me sit and type away, Tony, for the sauce!

Holly the pixies and The DVDA crew.

Jonny, my wonderful agent who has always believed and is also my friend.

For everyone who helped me cook and talked recipes – John W, Ricky and Prince Dhruv.

Everyone at MasterChef, especially Karen, The Daves, Nozzer, John Gilbert and Mister Wallace who all believed!

To my brilliant publishers Simon & Schuster Illustrated, Kerr, Francine, Ami and the wonderful Nicky – thank you for loving my title and getting me completely!

Lou Plank, THE best PR but also a true friend, and your Steve for testing.

Jonathan Conway, you're a star.

The Book Dream Team – Chris Terry, Danny, Miranda, Polly, Justine, Super Rich, Karen and Abi.

My nieces, nephew, godchildren and friends who have tasted and tested and tried!

To Betty, Nannie, Norman and Lely, even though you're no longer with me, for the recipes and food memories that inspired me.

And, for everything... Mummy and Billie. *xxx*

Also thanks to Magimix, Kin Knives, KitchenAid, Green & Black's, Weight Watchers, Clinique, Bobbi Brown and Dermalogica.

Props: The Dining Room Shop, www.thediningroomshop.co.uk

Pimpernel & Partners, www.pimpernelandpartners.co.uk